KITCHENS
How to

Real People – Real Projects™

HOMETIME®

Publisher: Dean Johnson
Editor: Pamela S. Price
Writer: Joseph Truini
Art Director: Bill Nelson
Copy Editor: Lisa Wagner

Hometime Hosts: Dean Johnson, Robin Hartl
Project Producer: Chris Balamut
Construction: Dean Doying, Dan Laabs
Technical review: Mark Kimball

Illustrator: Mario Ferro
Photographer: Jeff Lyman
Cover Photo: Maki Strunc Photography
Location Photography Manager: Michael Klaers
Studio Photography Manager: Jason Adair
Video Frame Capture: Julie Wallace

Production Coordinator: Pam Scheunemann
Electronic Layout: Chris Long

Book Creative Direction, Design and Production:
MacLean & Tuminelly, Minneapolis, MN
Cover Design: Richard Scales Advertising Associates

Library of Congress Catalog Card Number
96-80444
ISBN 1-890257-01-X

H O M E T I M E®
4275 Norex Drive
Chaska, MN 55318

Special Thanks: Jack McCarthy, McCarthy Plumbing;
Kate Hilgenberg, Jerry's Floor Store;
Bob Dempsey, Congoleum Corporation; Terry
Fitzpatrick, Mannington Resilent Floors; Sue Trotter,
Maycor; Scott Wise, Armstrong World Industries

Contributing Photography: Amana Refrigeration,
American Woodmark, Angelo Lighting Company,
Armstrong World Industries, Avonite, Broan Mfg.
Co., Bruce Hardwood Floors, Cold Spring Granite,
Congoleum, Florida Tile, General Electric,
Halo/Cooper Lighting, Hollingsworth, Kohler
Company, Merillat Industries, Plato Woodwork,
Sub-Zero, Whirlpool, Wilsonart, Viking Range

The work and procedures shown and described in
this book are intended for use by people having
average skills and knowledge of the subjects.
If you are inexperienced in using any of the tools,
equipment, or procedures depicted or described,
or think that the work and procedures shown and
described in this book may not be safe in your
chosen situation, consult a person skilled in the
performance of the work or procedure. Throughout this book there are specific safety recommenda-
tions. Pay careful attention to each of these.

The makers of this book disclaim any liability
for injury or damage arising out of any failure or
omission to perform the work or procedures shown
and described in this book. Your performance is at
your own risk.

Printed in the United States
Electronic Prepress: Encore Color Group
Printed by: Quebecor Printing

5 4 3   02 01 00 99 98

*For online project help and information on other
Hometime products, visit us on the Web at*
www.hometime.com

Introduction

One question Robin and I hear a lot is: Aren't you going to run out of project ideas? All we can say is, not as long as houses have kitchens. Kitchen remodeling has been – and remains – one of the most popular home improvement projects around. While it can be expensive, it offers perhaps the best return on investment of any home improvement project.

Beyond the finances, though, are other less tangible rewards. More and more, families spend time together in the kitchen and nearby great room. Entertaining has become more casual and it usually centers around the kitchen, too. Remodeling this space to make it more comfortable and efficient makes the time we spend there all the more enjoyable – reason enough to take on the project.

Here at Hometime we've remodeled at least a dozen kitchens. Each one has been unique and has presented its own set of design and construction challenges. We've covered all the basics in this book. Read it carefully before you tackle your project. It will help you handle most of the challenges you'll encounter in your own remodeling project. However, since kitchens are unique, you may run into something we haven't covered. Check out other resources: books, videos, the Internet, contractors, and your local building department will all offer solutions you can adapt to suit your situation.

Plan thoroughly, work safely, and when you're into that third week of microwave dinners and take-out pizzas, just remember that it will all be worth it when you're done!

Table of Contents

PLANNING and DESIGN

The planning-and-design phase of a new kitchen is, in many ways, the most important part of the entire project. A well-conceived plan will guide you through each step of the process and help ensure that work progresses smoothly and stays within your budget – two challenges you'll encounter many times throughout the renovation.

Planning your new kitchen starts with listing what you like and dislike about your present kitchen. Now is the time to confront – and correct – the demons and design flaws of your existing kitchen.

Needs Assessment

Evaluating the strengths and weaknesses of your present kitchen, as well as your family's lifestyle, is a crucial step in designing the new space. Resist the temptation to skip this step.

What's wrong?

The first question to ask is, "What's wrong with my kitchen?" List all the things you don't like, including both major problems and small annoyances.

To create a thorough list, leave a pad and pencil on the countertop for a week or so. Encourage all family members to jot down ideas as they occur.

It's also a good idea to list all the things that you do like in your present kitchen. Even if it's a short list, it's smart to identify any worthwhile features so you'll remember to incorporate them into the new design.

Before. *The problems with this kitchen may be all too familiar to you.*
- *Space is too small for two cooks.*
- *Kitchen is isolated from the rest of the house.*
- *Cabinets are outdated and don't provide enough storage by today's standards.*
- *No storage for recyclables.*
- *Countertops and flooring are worn and outdated.*
- *Too few electrical receptacles.*
- *Poor lighting.*
- *Not enough daylight.*
- *Poor ventilation.*

In a spacious kitchen *an island can help fill up unused floor space and shorten distances between work stations – a real benefit for two-cook kitchens.*

Is an island right for your kitchen?

Building an island is a great way to add storage and work space to a kitchen. Keep in mind, however, that not every kitchen can accommodate an island.

You should allow 42 inches between the island and the nearest countertop. For two-cook kitchens, expand the work aisle to 48 inches.

The recommended walkway width between an island and wall is 36 inches. Therefore, even a 2-foot-wide island requires an area that's about 9 feet wide.

Placement of the island is equally important. It should never block or interrupt the traffic pattern through the kitchen.

If you can't decide whether – or where – to install an island, try this: Mock up an island out of cardboard boxes and live with it for a few days. It'll soon become evident if you need to alter the size or position of the island.

Wishful thinking

This is the fun part of the planning process: Creating a wish list of all the items you want in your new kitchen. It doesn't cost anything to dream, so don't worry about the budget for now – that'll become a reality soon enough. Instead, concentrate on designing the best kitchen possible. You can always scale it back later as the final design takes shape.

It's not surprising that most wish lists start with new cabinets, countertops, and appliances. A majority of your time – and money – will go toward selecting components from these three categories.

Other popular wish-list items include enlarging the kitchen, adding an island or peninsula, making room for a dining table or eat-at counter, and removing a wall to open up the kitchen to an adjacent dining room.

After. We included some inconspicuous but rewarding upgrades in this kitchen. Here are some other ideas to consider for your new kitchen:

- Second sink
- Built-in spice rack
- Ceramic tile backsplash
- Pull-out trash can
- Roll-out shelves
- Recycling bins
- Pantry cabinet
- Telephone center with desk and file drawers
- Island cooktop or sink
- Wine rack
- Glass-panel doors on upper cabinets
- Baking center
- Open shelves for cookbooks
- Appliance garage
- Undercabinet lighting
- Open display shelves

Universal design

Most kitchens are designed to accommodate the average person, that is, an able-bodied, non-elderly adult. The problem is that this description fits less than 15 percent of the population. The goal of universal design is to create safe, accessible kitchens for everyone, regardless of physical ability, age, stature, or lifestyle.

Universal design was born of the needs of our changing society. Elderly and physically-challenged people are more independent than ever before. Shifting family roles are putting more fathers and teenagers in the kitchen. Plus, a growing number of three-generation households require flexible kitchen designs to accommodate cooks of all ages, sizes, and physical capabilities.

For more information on universal design, contact:
Center for Universal Design
(800/647-6777)
National Kitchen and Bath Association
(800/843-6522, ask for the UD guidelines)
U.S. Access Board
(800/872-2253)

Universal design elements in this kitchen include: handles instead of knobs on cabinets, a variable-height sink, knee space under the sink and cooktop, a contrasting-color edge band on the countertop, and spring-loaded, drop-down shelves.

Plans

The importance of having a detailed kitchen plan can't be overstated. It's the reference point from which all work is done, products are specified, and bids are offered. Without a plan, your dream – and budget – will crumble.

You can draw a plan from scratch, use a design aid (such as a planning kit), or hire a professional designer.

Drawing a kitchen plan

You don't have to be a skilled draftsperson or an architect to draw a kitchen plan. All you need are a few basic drawing instruments and measuring tools, such as a pencil, ruler, tape measure, and some ¼-inch-scale graph paper.

Begin by making a freehand sketch of your present kitchen floor plan that shows the layout of the walls. Next, carefully measure the length of the walls all the way around the room, noting the dimensions on the sketch. Then measure and mark the locations of all doors, windows, alcoves, and other permanent fixtures.

Once you've recorded these critical measurements, you're ready to make a more precise drawing on graph paper. Using your sketch as a reference, draw the floor plan in ¼-inch scale.

Draw all the walls, windows, and doors, but not the cabinets, counters, or appliances. After the basic floor plan is completed, take it into the kitchen and check each dimension again. If all the numbers add up, go ahead and make several photocopies of the drawing.

Now use either a drafting template or scraps of paper cut to size (look in manufacturers' catalogs for standard cabinets and appliance sizes) to try different layouts for the cabinets and appliances. This part of the pro-

Kitchen design guidelines

The National Kitchen and Bath Association has established specific rules to help professional designers and architects produce safe, functional, and space-efficient kitchens. Highlighted here are twelve of the NKBA's forty design guidelines.

Traffic and work flow
- Walkways between walls and counters or appliances must be at least 36 inches wide.
- Work aisles between two counters or a counter and appliance should be 42 inches wide; 48 inches for two-cook kitchens.
- Work triangles, measuring from sink to range to refrigerator, should not exceed a total of 26 feet. No one leg of the triangle should be shorter than 4 feet or longer than 9 feet.

Cabinets and storage
- Kitchens under 150 square feet should have 12 feet of wall cabinets and 13 feet of base cabinets.
- Kitchens larger than 150 square feet should have 15½ feet of wall cabinets and 16 feet of base cabinets.
- Two waste receptacles should be included, one for garbage and another for recyclables.

Appliance placement
- A 30- by 48-inch area of clear floor space must be provided in front of the sink, dishwasher, cooktop, oven, and refrigerator.
- The dishwasher should be within 36 inches of the primary sink.
- Microwave ovens should be placed 24 to 48 inches above the floor.

Counter surface
- Kitchens under 150 square feet should have at least 11 feet of countertop.
- Kitchens larger than 150 square feet should have 16½ feet of countertop.
- There should be 24 inches of counter to one side of the sink and 18 inches to the other.

For the complete design guidelines and other kitchen design and remodeling information, visit the NKBA Web site at www.nkba.org.

cess is a lot of fun, so don't be surprised if you end up with four or five designs to pick from.

Once you have the final design, make several copies of it. You'll need copies for the local building department, any contractors you ask to submit bids, kitchen showroom staff, designers, and other professionals.

Seeking professional help

Having trouble visualizing your dream kitchen? You may want to enlist the help of a professional. Design services are available from architects, kitchen designers, remodeling contractors, and most home centers.

Most architects and kitchen designers will not only design the kitchen, but will also manage the entire remodeling project if you wish. You'll pay for that additional service, but it'll save you the headache of dealing with the contractors and keeping the job – and the budget – on schedule.

A good choice in remodeling contractors is someone who owns a design/build firm. As the name implies, these contractors do both the designing and construction, but some will perform just the design aspect and leave the construction to you.

You can also find reliable (and often, free) information at kitchen showrooms and design centers in home centers and lumberyards.

Regardless of where you go for help, be sure to hire someone who specializes in kitchens. This is especially important when dealing with an architect or remodeling con-

tractor – you don't want someone who's only dabbling in kitchen design. And don't ever hire anyone without first checking references and seeing their past work.

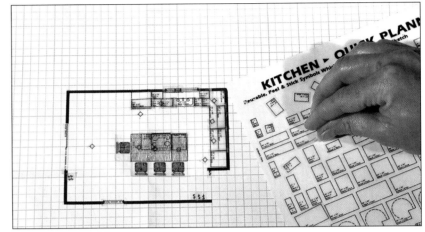

Kitchen design kits are sold at most home centers and hardware stores. They consist of a plastic-coated board that's printed with a ¼-inch-scale grid, and dozens of precut, cling-stick plastic templates. You simply stick the templates onto the board to create a design. The disadvantage of this type of product is that you can only create one design at a time.

3-D design programs allow you to create a design, then view it from all angles. Other useful features include libraries of cabinet, countertop, and flooring options, as well as estimating tools that allow you to see the effect of your design choices on your budget.

How to read an architect's rule

The trick to reading an architect's rule is to remember that each edge shows two scales: One reads right to left, the other, left to right.

To use the rule, match the scale on the rule to the scale indicated on the blueprint. Line up a foot marker to one end of the line you're measuring, then count the number of hash marks to the other side of the zero mark to determine the number of inches. (It's much less confusing than it sounds, honest.)

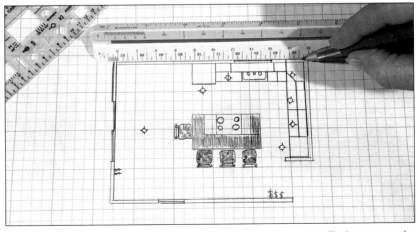

Blueprints, floor plans, and construction diagrams are typically drawn to scale. Each foot of actual space is reduced proportionately. Most kitchen plans are ¼-inch scale (¼ inch on the drawing equals one foot of kitchen space). If your kitchen is small enough, draw it to ½-inch scale. That'll make it easier to draw small details and odd-size dimensions more accurately.

Basic Floor Plans

There are millions of kitchens and no two look exactly alike. However, all kitchens are based on one of four basic kitchen layouts: L-shaped, U-shaped, galley, and one-wall.

L-shaped

The L-shaped kitchen is the most common kitchen layout. The longer wall often houses the range and sink; the end of the short wall is typically punctuated by the refrigerator.

A benefit of this layout is that the work triangle is uninterrupted by traffic flowing through the kitchen. The only notable drawback to an L-shaped layout is that large chunks of space are gobbled up by the range, refrigerator, and dishwasher. In smaller kitchens, that can create a shortage of base-cabinet storage. Two possible solutions are to add storage cabinets by lengthening one leg of the L or to build a peninsula.

U-shaped

In an average-sized kitchen, this design creates a compact work triangle that saves steps. Plus, it's well protected from through traffic, an important consideration for busy families with active children.

The one situation where a U-shaped layout doesn't work as well is in a large kitchen. The extended distances of the work triangle can make cooking feel like a real workout.

Galley

The galley kitchen is very efficient. However, galley kitchens are often short on counter space and can feel a little cramped, especially with two cooks.

Another concern is if there's a doorway at each end of the kitchen, then traffic will flow through the work triangle. You could block off one doorway to eliminate through traffic, but that creates a dead end that often makes a small space seem even smaller.

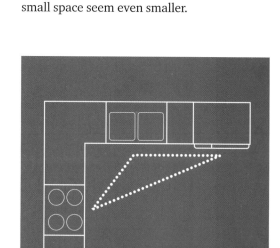

The L-shape *typically has one long leg and one slightly shorter leg. This right-angle arrangement is especially well-suited for kitchens that open up into an adjoining room.*

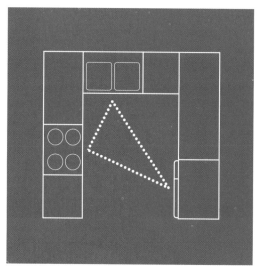

The U-shape *works well in mid-sized kitchens. With cabinets placed along three walls, the U-shaped layout surrounds you with cabinetry and appliances and provides plenty of accessible storage space.*

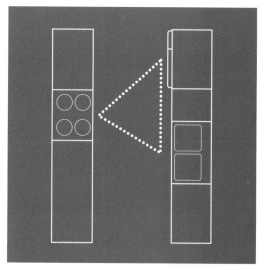

The galley, *or corridor, layout is ideally suited for narrow kitchens. Placing cabinets and appliances along opposite walls makes an efficient work triangle.*

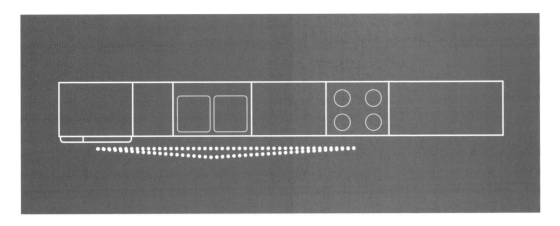

One-wall layouts are typically found in apartments and condominiums, but they're also ideal for in-law suites, vacation cottages, and other light-use kitchens. The main drawback is that counter and storage space is severely limited.

One-wall

The simplest of all kitchen layouts is spread along one wall. It may not be the most interesting design, but it does provide an effective way to squeeze in a kitchen without sacrificing a lot of floor space.

Unfortunately, it flattens the work triangle which forces you to trek back and forth from one end of the kitchen to the other. You can save steps by putting the sink in the center of the counter.

L-shaped with peninsula

Add storage and counter space to an L-shaped kitchen with a peninsula that protrudes out into the open floor and is accessible from both sides. This also creates an ideal spot for an eat-at counter; just widen the peninsula counter so it overhangs the cabinets on the back side by about 14 inches.

This hybrid layout is an excellent choice for two-cook families, especially when the peninsula has a cooktop or secondary sink. This arrangement creates two adjoining work triangles so two people can work together at the same time, in the same space, with little interference.

U-shaped with island

This is perhaps the most desirable layout of all and it's easy to see why: It's a spacious plan that offers ample storage cabinets, plenty of countertop, and an endless array of design options. In a large kitchen, installing an island that houses a sink or cooktop is a sure-fire way to shorten distances.

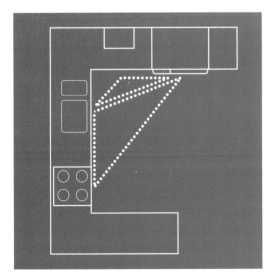

Adding a peninsula to an L-shaped kitchen is one of the easiest, most economical ways to gain extra counter and cabinet space. It then essentially becomes a U-shaped layout positioned along two walls.

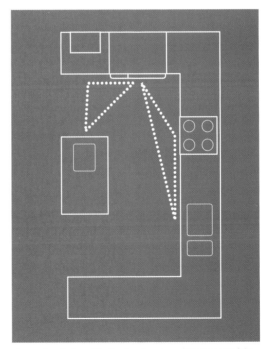

A center island helps to shorten distances in big U-shaped kitchens. It can also transform a large, open area into an efficient work space for two cooks. A popular island amenity is a storage bin for recyclables.

Construction Planning

Once you have a drawing of the kitchen, you're ready for the all-important construction planning phase. Now is the time to establish a budget, pull building permits, decide how much work you'll do yourself, and set a construction timetable. You also need to think about what to do with demolition debris and where to store building materials.

Establishing a budget

There's no magic formula to follow when it comes to estimating a new kitchen. However, you can get an accurate estimate by breaking down the project into smaller jobs.

Start by getting prices on all new products. To find the exact styles, colors, and models that you like, visit showrooms, home centers, and building suppliers, talk to designers, and look through manufacturers' catalogs. When you ask for prices, make sure to ask about delivery charges, taxes, and other hidden costs. Usually, about 45 percent of your budget will go toward new cabinets; counters and appliances will each claim another 10 percent.

The next step is to get estimates for any work that you won't be doing yourself. Obtain itemized, written quotes from at least three licensed contractors. If the work includes providing building materials, be sure that they're specified in writing. That way, you'll be comparing the estimates accurately.

Finally, add up all the numbers and tack on an additional 20 percent for cost overruns. If the final figure is more than you wish

Budget busters

Each step of the remodeling process is a minefield of hidden costs just waiting to blow the lid off your budget.

The biggest budget busters of all are change orders. That's when you make a change to the original plan after construction has begun. Sometimes a change order is unavoidable, such as when demolition reveals underlying structural problems. But, whenever possible, avoid luxury change orders by making a solid construction plan and sticking to it.

A close relative to the change order is while-you're-at-it syndrome. That's when you take on additional projects, simply because you're in the remodeling mode. It's tough enough to stay within the budget you've planned – don't go looking for trouble.

Here are several other factors that can break a budget:
- Permit fees.
- Order mix-ups.
- Repairing accidental damage to floors, walls, and doors.
- Landfill drop-off fees.
- Renting or buying specialty tools.
- Upgrading the kitchen's electrical service.
- Shipping delays due to bad weather, out-of-stock items, holidays, and labor strikes.

Build flexibility into the budget by scouting out less expensive alternatives as you select products for your new kitchen. Those B-list items will provide some flexibility should your budget get squeezed by an unanticipated expense. For example, substituting a stone-look plastic-laminate countertop (right) for a granite countertop (left) provides a similar effect at a fraction of the cost.

to spend, start cutting back by substituting items. For example, switch from custom cabinets to stock, or choose vinyl flooring instead of ceramic tile.

Do-it-yourself

The best way to control construction costs is to do as much of the work yourself as possible. Your degree of participation depends upon your skill level, your remodeling experience and, perhaps most importantly, your spare time. The most common mistake do-it-yourselfers make is underestimating how long it takes to complete a project.

Check the local building codes to see if you're allowed to do your own plumbing and electrical work. Some local building codes only allow licensed professionals to do this work.

Even novice do-it-yourselfers can reduce costs significantly just by handling demolition, clean-up, patching and painting, and hanging wallpaper.

Order of events

All kitchen remodeling projects follow a logical work sequence. Your project might not encompass all of the jobs listed below, but it'll follow a similar order.

The times shown represent eight-hour work days. That is, only the actual working time is listed, not the hours eaten up by shipping delays, waiting for inspections, design changes, or countless trips to the hardware store.

Job	Time
Prepare the room	1 day
Demolition	1 to 2 days
Mechanical rough-ins	2 to 3 days
Hang new cabinets	2 to 3 days
Fabricate and set new counters	2 to 3 days
Lay new flooring	2 to 3 days
Install sink and faucet	1 day
Hook up appliances	1 to 2 days
Install light fixtures	1 to 2 days
Trim-out	1 to 2 days
Final cleanup	1 day

Permits and inspections

Before starting construction, take your kitchen plans to the local building department and apply for a building permit. An inspector will review the plans before granting the permit, a process that could take anywhere from a few days to a few weeks. Sepa-

Each bid should contain an itemized list of materials and project steps. That makes it easier to compare bids and creates a better understanding between you and the contractor as to what the job will and will not include.

rate permits are usually required for building, plumbing, electrical, and heating.

The building inspector also performs scheduled inspections to ensure that all work is done according to code. Ask for an inspection schedule and be sure to get required inspection sign-offs before proceeding to the

How to hire a competent contractor

- Ask friends, neighbors, and architects for the names of contractors they've used.
- Get at least three written estimates with itemized labor and materials costs for all work.
- Don't be tempted by very low bids. (If it seems too good to be true, it probably is.)
- Insist on fixed-price bids; if you agree to pay an hourly rate, the job may never end.
- Speak with the contractor's past clients. Ask if they were pleased with the quality of the work, if the job was finished on time, and if it was easy to communicate with the contractor. Whenever possible, go see the finished projects for yourself.
- Investigate the contractor's bank references and credit history.
- Find out which building suppliers the contractor uses and call to see if bills are paid regularly.
- Be sure that all hired help is bonded, insured, and licensed. Make sure the contractor carries both liability and workers compensation insurance. Find out if the documents are up-to-date and valid.
- Check out each prospective contractor with your local consumer affairs office, the Better Business Bureau, and local trade associations. Make sure there are no complaints on file against the contractor.
- Maintain control of the job by controlling the money. Make lump-sum payments only for completed work. Get signed lien waivers from the contractor and all subs who work on the job.

next project step. Inspections are typically required for:

- Rough mechanicals, including plumbing, electrical, and heating.
- Framing for walls, windows, doors, and floors.
- Insulation in walls, floors, and ceilings.
- Drywall (before taping the joints).
- Final inspection of the completed kitchen.

Solving the debris dilemma

Don't forget to plan ahead for the mountain of debris that'll be created during demolition. The smartest solution is to recycle whatever you can, including cardboard boxes, copper pipes, even old cabinets and plumbing fixtures.

To handle the remaining debris, rent a dumpster. Have it dropped as close to the kitchen as possible, but keep in mind that if the container is placed on the lawn, it can kill the grass. If it's set down on a warm asphalt driveway, it may sink in. You might be able to park the container at the curb, but first check with the local police.

An alternative to renting a dumpster is to pile the debris in the driveway. Then hire a hauler to come pick it all up when the project is done.

Staging materials

A detail that's often overlooked is where to store all the cabinets, lumber, flooring, and other materials when they arrive. An attached garage provides an ideal warehouse, but not all homes have attached garages. If that's the case at your home, devote a room near the kitchen for storage. Be sure to protect the walls and floor.

There is one more point to consider. Guess who's responsible for damage or theft of materials at the jobsite: The delivery company? Nope. The contractor? Not likely. You? Bingo.

Call your insurance agent and ask if your homeowner's policy covers stockpiled building materials. Chances are it will only cover materials once they are attached to the house, so look into buying additional coverage for the next couple of months.

Surviving a kitchen remodeling

Are you prepared to live without a functioning kitchen for a few weeks – maybe even a couple of months? Can you imagine scavenging through cardboard boxes for your favorite coffee mug, microwaving entire meals, and washing dishes in the bathtub? Those are the realities of daily life when your kitchen is under construction.

While no one enjoys roughing it in their own home, it is possible to survive a remodeling with a minimal amount of inconvenience and disruption – but only if you plan ahead.

First, set up a temporary kitchen in an adjoining room using a few of the old base cabinets and a long section of countertop.

Pack up all but the most essential kitchen items and store them in the garage or basement. Steamer trunks and large suitcases can be used as dust-free storage boxes for nonessential dishes, pots, and pans.

Find a spot in the provisional kitchen for the refrigerator, coffee maker, and trash can. If the range is going to be out of commission for an extended period, plan your meals around the microwave, electric skillet, toaster oven, and barbecue grill. Of course, eating out at restaurants is an option, but only if you've budgeted for it.

Also be aware of any upcoming holidays. Make arrangements to dine with relatives or friends. Finally, don't create any additional pressure by planning a party in your new kitchen – until it's completely finished. Unrealistic goals and rigid deadlines can ruin even the best laid remodeling schemes.

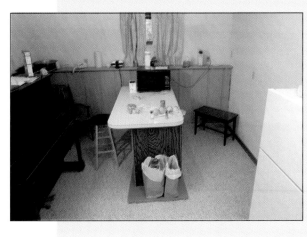

How long can you live like this? Careful planning can make it bearable – at least for a while. Buy or borrow a hot plate, toaster oven, and/or Crock-Pot to supplement the microwave. Check specialty cookbooks for one-pot meals, grilling tips, and interesting sandwiches.

BUYER'S GUIDE to KITCHEN PRODUCTS

Before diving into the hands-on portion of the project, you must first choose cabinets, countertops, appliances, and other products for your new kitchen.

To avoid shop-'til-you-drop syndrome, do your homework before hitting the road. Look through home-improvement magazines and decorating books. Study product catalogs. Attend a home-remodeling show. Then visit kitchen showrooms, home centers, appliance stores, lighting dealers, and plumbing suppliers to inspect each product you're considering.

Take along a notebook to jot down model numbers, colors, sizes, and prices. Also find out how long it'll take for each product to be delivered once you place the order; factor these shipping times into your construction schedule.

Cabinets

To the average person, all kitchen cabinets might look pretty much the same. But quality (like price) varies widely – even when comparing cabinets from the same manufacturer. That's why it's important to look beyond the styling and focus on the quality of the construction.

Judging quality

When comparing cabinets, there are three areas to examine: casework, drawers, and hardware.

The case (also called the carcass or carcase) is usually built of either plywood or particleboard. Plywood holds nails and screws better, and is less susceptible to swelling. However, particleboard is the better substrate for plastic laminate.

The best drawers are made of solid wood with a plywood bottom. Drawers entirely made of plywood come in a close second, but steer clear of particleboard drawers – they just won't stand up to daily use.

How the drawer parts are joined together is as important as what they're made from. Dovetailed construction creates the strongest, longest-lasting drawers. Rabbet and doweled butt joints are not quite as strong, but are more than adequate for most kitchens.

Hardware is another good barometer of quality. Look for doors that swing open beyond 90 degrees. Make sure the hinges are fully adjustable so you can keep the doors evenly spaced and aligned. Full-extension drawer slides allow the full depth of the drawer to slide out of the cabinet so you can easily access items in the back of the drawer.

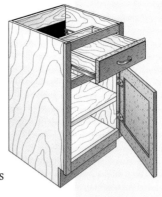

Framed vs. frameless

Kitchen cabinets come in hundreds of styles, but in only two basic types: framed and frameless. Framed cabinets have a face frame attached to the front of the cabinet. The frame accepts a wide range of hinges, including surface-mounted, partially concealed, and fully concealed.

With frameless, or European-style, cabinets, the doors are hung directly from the sides of the case with fully concealed hinges. With no frame to block the opening of the box, frameless units offer easier access to the interior of the cabinet. Frameless cabinets are generally considered to be more difficult to install.

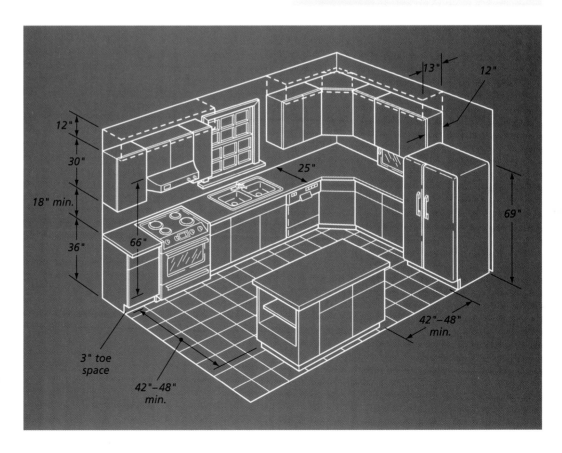

Measurements that have become standards in kitchen layout include 25-inch-deep counters, 30-inch-tall wall cabinets, and 13-inch-deep soffits. An island requires 42 inches between it and the nearest countertop; expand that to 48 inches for a two-cook kitchen.

Stock, custom, or semi-custom?

Kitchen cabinet manufacturers offer three distinct lines of cabinetry: stock, custom, and semi-custom.

Stock cabinets are the most affordable of the three. They're mass-produced in standard sizes and kept in stock at local distributors and retailers. The result is fast delivery, often in less than a week.

Stock cabinets are made in 3-inch increments ranging from 9-inches wide to 48-inches wide. By mixing and matching cabinets of various widths, you can create a run of cabinetry that comes within a few inches of filling up an entire kitchen wall. The remaining gap is hidden by a matching filler strip.

Custom cabinets have no standard sizes. Each one is made to your exact specifications. As you may have guessed, this is an expensive option, but it's the best choice for optimum design flexibility. Delivery time for custom cabinets is a minimum of six to eight weeks.

Semi-stock cabinets are a hybrid of stock and custom cabinets. They come in standard widths, but offer many more choices than stock cabinets, including a greater number of cabinet styles, door designs, drawer options, decorative finishes, and storage accessories. Allow at least four to six weeks shipping time for semi-custom cabinets.

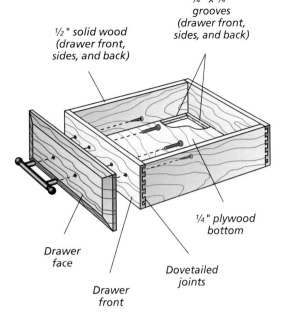

½" solid wood (drawer front, sides, and back)

¼" x ¼" grooves (drawer front, sides, and back)

¼" plywood bottom

Drawer face

Drawer front

Dovetailed joints

Cabinet drawers reveal *more about quality construction than any other single component, including price. Quality drawer construction features dovetail joints, a separate drawer face, and a plywood bottom held in grooves.*

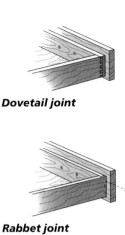

Dovetail joint

Rabbet joint

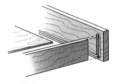

Dowel joint

Butt joint

Which line of cabinets is right for you? That may depend on your budget. Semi-custom cabinets generally cost about 25 percent more than stock units; custom cabinets range anywhere from 30 percent to 100 percent more than semi-custom.

Customizing stock cabinets

Most cabinet companies offer a line of optional accessories that allows you to tailor your stock cabinets to meet your specific storage needs. Options include roll-out shelves, pivoting pantry units, recycling bins, wine racks, appliance garages, spice racks, and pop-up shelves for electric mixers.

You can order specialty hardware when you order the cabinets, or you can buy the hardware separately and install it yourself after the cabinets are in place.

Recycling bins *hung from a rotating frame make good use of the often-wasted space in a corner cabinet.*

Pull-out shelves *make it easier to find and reach items stored at the back of the cabinet.*

Storing knives *loose in a drawer is dangerous, as well as bad for the blades. This unit provides safe storage for knives plus a pull-out cutting board.*

Frame-and-panel doors are available with flat, or recessed, panels (left) or with classic raised panels (middle). Most door panels are cut straight across the top, but they also come in cathedral-style which has arched or belled tops (right).

Inset doors

An inset door is a traditional design. It differs from other door styles because it fits within, not over, the cabinet's face frame.

Inset doors are only available on high-end custom cabinets. In fact, many manufacturers don't even offer inset doors because they're time-consuming and costly to build. The doors must fit precisely into perfectly square face frames to create an even gap

around each door. If you're considering cabinets with inset doors, be sure they're equipped with fully adjustable hinges.

Door styles

From Shaker to Gothic, Colonial to French Country, the architectural style of a kitchen cabinet is based almost entirely on the design of its doors. Cabinet doors come in two basic types: frame-and-panel and flush-panel.

A typical frame-and-panel door has a four-part solid wood frame surrounding a solid wood or plywood panel. In a traditional frame-and-panel door, the panel floats (meaning it's not glued) in grooves cut in the frame. This allows the panel to expand and contract without splitting. Modern frame-and-panel doors, however, are often made from processed-wood substrates, such as particleboard or medium-density fiberboard (MDF), and then covered with a vinyl skin.

Flush-panel doors, also called slab doors, are often chosen for contemporary-style kitchens. They're simply a flat piece of ⅝-inch- or ¾-inch-thick plywood or processed-wood substrate that's covered with wood veneer, plastic laminate, or vinyl. Flush-panel doors generally come in a wider selection of colors than framed doors, but framed doors are available in a greater array of natural and stained wood-grain finishes.

When choosing a door style, be aware that there are two primary ways that a door is sized to fit the cabinet: full overlay and partial overlay. A full-overlay door covers nearly the entire face frame or, in the case of a frameless unit, the edges of the cabinet.

There's often less than ⅛ inch reveal around the entire door.

A partial-overlay door is similar to a full-overlay door, only it's smaller. It permits about an inch of the face frame to show around the door's edges. Deciding between full-overlay and partial-overlay doors is mostly a matter of taste, but price can play a role, too: Partial-overlay cabinets often cost less simply because less material is used to make each door.

Cabinet finishes

There are four types of finish commonly used on the exterior of kitchen cabinets: stain, plastic laminate, paint, and thermofoil vinyl.

Stained finishes are the most popular and are found on wood and wood-veneer cabinets. They come in numerous semi-transparent wood tones and a handful of opaque pickled, or oatmeal, colors.

A clear topcoat finish, such as varnish or lacquer, is applied over the stain to seal out grime and provide an easy-to-clean surface. Look for cabinets finished with a catalyzed varnish that contains a UV sunblock; this will prevent the finish from fading and yellowing.

If you prefer the look of natural wood, order the cabinets with a varnish-only (no stain) finish. If you'd like to finish your own cabinets on site, shop around. Some manufacturers do sell their cabinets unfinished.

Plastic laminate is applied to particleboard

cabinets, particularly frameless units with flush-panel doors. One main benefit is that it comes in many colors, patterns, and textures, including simulated wood grain, stone, metal, and leather. Plastic laminate is also affordable, durable, and easy to clean. It's mostly used on stock cabinets and low-end semi-custom units.

Paint is a popular finish that gives you a choice of many colors. The main disadvantage of paint is that it chips and scratches easily. Plus, when applied to wood-framed doors, it tends to develop hairline cracks where the door stiles join the rails and also along the panel grooves.

For a painted look without the chips and cracks, consider thermofoil vinyl. In this process, a thin vinyl film (known as a foil) is pressure-laminated to an MDF core which has been routed to a specific profile, such as a raised-bevel panel. The result is a tough, seamless finish that cleans up easily.

Only the doors and drawer fronts are thermofoiled, however. The cabinet boxes are usually finished with paint, plastic laminate, or melamine. Color choices are severely limited – most manufacturers only offer thermofoil cabinets in basic white.

This flush-panel, full-overlay door is finished with plastic laminate; it's typically used on European-style frameless cabinets.

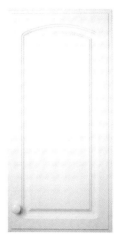

This thermofoil vinyl door has an MDF core, routed to resemble a traditional-looking, cathedral-style door.

Curved cabinetry provides an effective way to break up all the flat surfaces of a typical kitchen.

A diagonal-front corner wall cabinet makes better use of the space than a blind corner cabinet. The glass-panel door adds visual interest.

Special configurations

A straight run of cabinets all the same size may provide great storage, but it will also be visually uninteresting. Fortunately, all kinds of accessories and specialty units are available to customize both your storage and the look of your kitchen.

Among the options to consider are wine racks, open shelving, and glass-panel doors. Think, too, about adding trim moldings or valances along the tops of cabinets.

For ideas on using stock components to create custom shelving and specialty work areas, see page 53.

Countertop Options

A kitchen counter must survive years of abuse without looking worn or outdated. Here are five countertop materials that will meet, and often exceed, expectations.

Plastic laminate

Laminate is by far the most popular and affordable countertop material. If you have the tools and skills, you can make the countertop yourself. Plastic laminate is sold at home centers and lumberyards for about $2 to $3 per square foot; add in the other materials you need and you're looking at about $6.50 per linear foot to make your own countertop.

You could also hire a custom fabricator to make the counter; expect to pay from $25 to $50 per linear foot. If you're short of both time and money, consider a ready-made countertop. Two styles are sold at home centers: square-edge counter with separate backsplash ($16 or more per linear foot) and postformed top (about $7 per linear foot).

Ceramic tile

Available in virtually every color and unlimited patterns and textures, tile is the material for creating one-of-a-kind counters. It's durable, virtually scratchproof, and extremely heat resistant. Keeping the grout joints clean can be a challenge, however.

This square-edged plastic-laminate countertop has a ¾-inch-thick particleboard substrate; the edges are built up to 1½ inches.

Ready-made postformed countertops have seamless construction because they are heat-molded from a single sheet of plastic laminate. They come with an integral backsplash.

Bullnose tiles overlap the front edge tiles in this common ceramic tile edge treatment.

Hardwood trim is easy to install, but must be refinished periodically, especially the area right in front of the sink.

Counter trim, or V-cap, tiles have a no-drip design that prevents spilled liquids from running off the counter.

Solid-surface material comes in dozens of colors and an array of stone patterns. Different colors and patterns can be seamlessly fused together to create custom edge treatments and inlays.

Setting a ceramic-tile counter is within the capabilities of most do-it-yourselfers. Tile prices range widely, but start at around $3 per square foot.

Solid-surface material

Solid-surface material is made of acrylic and/or polyester, but resembles marble or granite. The color is solid throughout so scratches and burns can be sanded out.

Unfortunately, this is not a do-it-yourself product; fabrication requires specialized tools and techniques. A standard 25-inch-deep counter with 4-inch backsplash will cost about $100 to $175 per linear foot, installed.

Granite

Granite comes in nearly three dozen colors including pink, black, gray, green, and blue. It's also expensive: $150 to $200 per linear foot.

The counters are usually 1½ inches thick and extremely heavy. Installation is best left to a professional. For a more affordable, do-it-yourself granite counter, consider granite tiles (about $15 to $20 per square foot).

Wood

Butcherblock countertops are made up of strips or blocks of solid maple or red oak, and

Granite countertops are heat-resistant, impervious to stains and scratches, waterproof, and virtually indestructible.

Butcherblock counters are available in end-, edge-, and face-grain configurations. End-grain butcherblocks are stronger, but also more expensive.

finished with either oil or urethane. The disadvantage of a wood counter is that you can't neglect the maintenance, especially around the sink. A butcherblock counter must be kept dry and well sealed to avoid cracking.

Butcherblock costs about $50 per linear foot, and installation requires only a few standard carpentry tools.

Solid-surface options

From shaped edges to elegant inlays, no material offers more design possibilities than a solid-surface counter.

The most popular detail is to shape the counter's front edge with a rounding-over, bullnose, chamfer, or Roman ogee bit. A fancier (and more expensive) option is to groove the edge for a strip of wood, brass, or steel. To create a striking effect, have a contrasting color strip fused to the edge or inlaid as pinstriping.

Looking to express an artistic bent? Then order a custom-crafted inlay. Virtually any design that you can dream up can be routed into the countertop and then filled with a tinted

liquid compound.

Solid-surface sinks are available in matching or contrasting colors. The sink bowl is fused to the counter's underside, then the opening is routed out. Another popular option is an integral drain board that's cut right into the countertop.

If you're going to invest in a solid-surface counter, heed this important rule: Hire an experienced, certified fabricator. That way you'll know that he or she has taken a manufacturer-sponsored training course and knows the proper way to cut, shape, and fuse the material.

A double-bowl, solid-surface sink is fused into place on the underside of the solid-surface countertop.

The sink opening is routed out. Be sure to ask the fabricator for the cutout piece – it makes a great cutting board.

A specially designed rounding-over bit is used to create a smooth transition between the counter and the sink.

A highly specialized router template is used for cutting an integral drain board into the countertop.

Appliances

There's a lot to consider when buying new appliances: style, color, price, size, energy costs. When comparing appliances, remember that while an energy-efficient model may cost more initially, the higher upfront cost is generally recovered in lower energy costs long before the appliance wears out.

Refrigerators

How big a refrigerator-freezer do you need? This depends on your family's lifestyle and eating habits. But, the general rule is a minimum of 8 to 10 cubic feet of refrigerator storage space for two people, plus another cubic foot for each additional person. Also add 2 cubic feet of freezer space per person.

A standard refrigerator is 27 to 32 inches deep, and sticks out past the cabinets by at least 3 inches. If you want a refrigerator that fits flush with the cabinets, choose either a built-in or a freestanding cabinet-depth model.

Ranges, cooktops, and ovens

Ranges combine a cooktop and oven in a single unit and come in three basic styles: freestanding, slide-in, and drop-in.

If you prefer, you could install a separate cooktop and wall oven instead of a range. That way, you can install the oven at any convenient height. To keep two cooks out of each other's way, install both a range and a separate cooktop. Add a wall oven, too, if you do a lot of baking and roasting.

Convection ovens are equipped with a fan that circulates heat for faster cooking. They also heat more evenly than radiant ovens, so they're excellent for baking.

Can't decide between gas and electric? Consider a dual-fuel arrangement that combines a gas cooktop and electric oven. You get the wide temperature range and quick response of a gas cooktop and the even heat of an electric oven.

The standard range is 30 inches wide, but

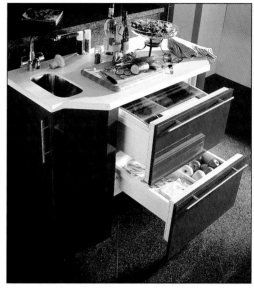

Under-the-counter refrigerator or freezer drawers keep food in the area it will be prepared – veggies near the sink, for example, and frozen goods near the microwave.

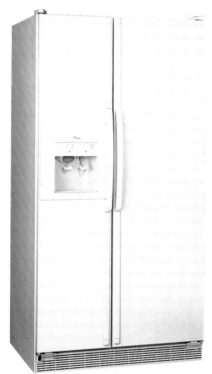

Side-by-side refrigerators range in size from about 20 cubic feet to 30 cubic feet. However, the narrow compartments may not accommodate large frozen pizzas or oversize platters.

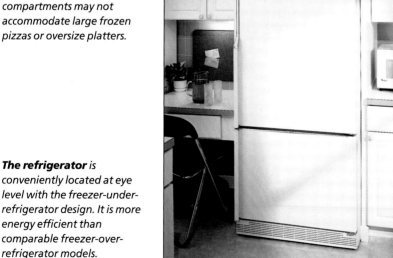

The refrigerator is conveniently located at eye level with the freezer-under-refrigerator design. It is more energy efficient than comparable freezer-over-refrigerator models.

Halogen cooktops generate heat with high-powered electric bulbs. They heat up faster than radiant cooktops, but cost about 50 percent more.

24- and 36-inch units are also available. Wall ovens are 24, 27, or 30 inches wide. Cooktops are commonly available in two widths: 30 and 36 inch.

Ventilation

Range hoods help keep the air clear of cooking odors, steam, and smoke. It is best to vent to the outdoors. If that's not an option in your kitchen, non-vented models are available.

Modular cooktops accept different types of plug-in modules, such as burners, grills, griddles, rotisseries, and woks. This unit has a grill and gas burners flanking a down-draft vent.

Low-profile, slide-out range hoods are only about 2 inches thick. The fan motor and duct are housed in the cabinet above.

(These draw air through a filter and then recirculate it back into the kitchen.)

Downdraft vents are mounted in between or just behind the cooking elements. This type of unit requires a more powerful – and noisier – fan motor than an overhead vent hood.

Dishwashers

Most dishwashers have three cleaning cycles. Additional cycles are available, but not essential. One worthwhile feature is a delay-start timer that lets you preset the dishwasher to go on after you've left for work or gone to bed. Some units still have porcelain-enameled metal interiors, but plastic or stainless-steel interiors last longer.

A standard dishwasher measures 24 inches wide by 24 inches deep.

This commercial-style range features large, high-output burners and easy-to-clean stainless-steel construction. Commercial-grade ranges are available up to 60 inches wide.

Microwave oven options

Microwave ovens are typically placed on the countertop, or on shelves integrated into the wall cabinets. Some models are designed to be installed above a range. That type of unit has an integral fan motor and cooking light so it doubles as range hood.

The microwave shown here is a combination microwave and convection oven, which cooks faster and more evenly than a standard microwave oven.

Flooring

Kitchen floors are expected to be durable, easy-to-clean, slip-resistant, and impervious to damp moppings. The most popular choices include wood, resilient vinyl, ceramic tile, and plastic laminate.

Wood

Wood flooring comes in solid and engineered versions, prefinished or unfinished, and in three basic styles: strip, plank, and parquet. Traditional hardwood strip flooring is up to 2¼ inches wide, and ¾ inch thick. Planks are 3 inches and wider. Wood parquet tiles are typically 12 inches square.

Prefinished flooring costs more than unfinished, but it eliminates the extra work, mess, and expense of sanding and varnishing on site. On the other hand, site-finishing offers the best chance to get an even finish across the entire floor. It is also the best bet if you're trying to match existing woodwork or flooring. While prefinished flooring comes from the factory with a consistent finish, matching touch-up work on site can be difficult.

Engineered flooring is made up of at least three plies: a ⅛-inch-thick hardwood top surface, a solid-wood crossband core, and veneer backing. It cannot be refinished as often as solid wood products. It is, however, more dimensionally stable than solid wood and less inclined to show gaps between boards as the seasons change.

Engineered flooring can be nailed or glued down, but the quickest, easiest installation is the floating-floor

The most water-resistant finishes for wood flooring are convertible finishes such as moisture-cure urethane and acid-cure Swedish finishes. With prefinished flooring, look for an acrylic-impregnated finish.

Choosing to install wood flooring is simple – it's choosing which wood flooring that's difficult. You must decide on strips, planks, or tiles; solid or engineered; domestic or exotic wood; prefinished or site-finished; stained or natural.

This honey-oak floor is actually vinyl strip flooring. Each 3-inch by 36-inch "board" is glued down individually.

method. The tongue-and-groove planks are simply glued together; they're not fastened to the subfloor in any way.

Plastic laminate

Plastic-laminate flooring was popular in Europe for years before it became available in the United States. Now, several European brands are readily available here, as well as many lines made by American manufacturers.

This flooring has a high-pressure plastic-laminate surface bonded to a particleboard or MDF core. The laminate used for flooring is much tougher than the laminate used for

Sheet vinyl flooring creates a seamless, easy-to-clean surface that's both durable and affordable.

countertops. It's available in woodgrain, marble, and granite patterns, as well as solid colors. The flooring is about ¼ inch thick and comes in 7-inch-wide by 4-foot-long planks and 16-inch-square tiles.

Plastic-laminate flooring won't fade in direct sunlight, and is highly stain-, dent-, and scratch-resistant.

Resilient vinyl

Resilient vinyl flooring comes in two basic forms: sheet and tile. Sheet flooring is available in 6- and 12-foot-wide rolls which means a seamless installation is possible in most kitchens. Vinyl tiles come in 9- and 12-inch squares with either a peel-and-stick adhesive backing or a plain back for gluing down with mastic.

There are also two types of sheet vinyl. Perimeter-bonded floors are stapled or glued down around the edge of the room and glued along any seams. Fully adhered flooring is

laid in a coat of mastic that's spread over the entire floor. The two types are similar in appearance, quality, and cost, but perimeter-bonded floors are easier to install. And, since they're not stuck down, they do a better job of hiding small imperfections in the surface below. Fully adhered vinyl, on the other hand, is less likely to tear, stretch, or bubble.

When comparing the cost of resilient flooring, keep in mind that sheet vinyl is priced by the square yard, while tiles are priced by the square foot.

Ceramic tile

Ceramic tile is an extremely durable floor material. It's available in a wide range of colors, sizes, patterns, and architectural styles. However, there are drawbacks: Tile is cold and hard underfoot, noisy, relatively expensive, and unforgiving to dropped breakables. Plus, the grout joints must be strictly maintained to prevent stains and cracks.

Glazed ceramic tile is the best choice for kitchen floors. Its kiln-fired glaze is impervious to staining and it's readily available in sizes from 1 inch to 24 inches square.

Quarry and porcelain tiles are unglazed. Their color is solid throughout the tile so chips and deep scratches are nearly undetectable. Unfortunately, these porous tiles are susceptible to staining. Sealer will help them resist stains, but will also make them slippery when wet.

Peel-and-stick tiles are the easiest vinyl flooring to install and repair, but dirt does tend to collect in the seams.

Glazed ceramic tile offers superior durability and unlimited design options. For the most slip resistance, choose tiles with a matte or textured finish.

Sinks

The most popular kitchen sinks are made of stainless steel and it's easy to understand why: They're affordable and virtually indestructible. However, stainless steel isn't perfect. It's noisy, not available in colors, and susceptible to water spots.

Porcelain-enameled cast-iron sinks are available in a broad range of colors and styles. Cast iron is dense and heavy which makes for a very quiet sink.

You can also buy a kitchen sink molded from solid-surface material in a variety of solid colors and simulated granite patterns. The material is stain-resistant, quiet, and forgiving to breakables.

Another important consideration when choosing a sink is how it mounts to the countertop. A self-rimming sink, with its rim supported by the counter, is the easiest to install. An under-mount sink fastens to the underside of the counter so spills and crumbs can be brushed right into the sink.

Faucets

When choosing a faucet, be sure that it's compatible with the sink (the sink must have the correct number of holes, properly spaced), and that replacement parts are readily available.

Large sinks require a long-neck faucet, one that's fitted with a swiveling aerator, or one of the pull-out sprayer/faucet models.

Goose-neck faucets are handy for filling tall pots and vases. Consider faucets with levers, which are easier to operate than knobs.

The baked-on finish of an enameled cast-iron sink stands up well to rough scrubbings and hot liquids, but it can chip if you hit it hard enough. Enameled cast-iron sinks are available in styles from traditional to modern.

Triple-bowl sinks can accommodate soaking, rinsing, and drying dishes, but require a large base cabinet. If you're considering a stainless steel sink, choose an 18-gauge model that has sound-deadening insulation.

To use this ergonomic palm sprayer you pull it straight out – no twisting involved. This reduces strain on the wrist, and on the hose.

The small basin on the right side of this self-rimming sink is attached to a disposer. The main bowl is large enough to easily hold large skillets and pots for cleaning.

Under-mount sinks allow great design flexibility. Pick bowls the size and shape you like and arrange them to suit your needs. Just remember that the faucet must reach into each bowl.

Lighting

Constantly working in your own shadow is not only annoying and tiring, but dangerous, too. Good kitchen lighting starts with a detailed plan and strategic placement of ambient, task, and accent lighting fixtures.

Ambient lighting

Ambient lighting is the general light used to illuminate the overall space. It's usually provided by some type of ceiling-mounted fixture, such as track lights, recessed can lights, or a hanging pendant light. For a softer, indirect glow, position the fixtures so they bounce light off a wall or ceiling.

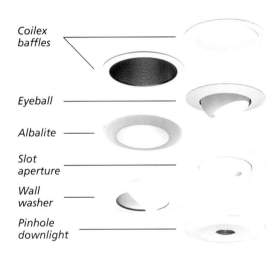

Coilex baffles

Eyeball

Albalite

Slot aperture

Wall washer

Pinhole downlight

Recessed light fixtures come in standard and compact sizes. Various trim kits help direct the light exactly where it's needed.

Task lighting

Task lighting is needed wherever you perform a specific job. Task lighting for a sink or range can be provided by a carefully aimed recessed ceiling fixture or halogen track lights.

The best way to brighten a countertop is with an undercabinet light. The most popular choices include thin fluorescent fixtures of various lengths and compact low-voltage halogen lights that come in two- or three-bulb strips. Both types are easy to install and energy efficient.

Accent lighting

Accent lighting is used to highlight a kitchen's special features. It's often placed inside a glass-door cabinet, alongside a display shelf, or behind crown molding running

along the tops of the upper cabinets.

For the inside of a cabinet, soffit, or recessed wall niche, the preferred option is a small circular halogen fixture that's commonly known as a hockey puck. Another popular accent-light option, known as star strips, is a band of tiny incandescent bulbs strung through a length of flexible clear tubing.

If budget restrictions prohibit you from adding accent lighting, try this trick: Install dimmer switches to a few ambient-light and task-light fixtures. You'll be able to adjust the light level and, in effect, create accent lighting.

The best lighting plans use a variety of strategically placed fixtures to produce even, balanced lighting and to eliminate dark shadows without creating glaring hot spots. To help accomplish those objectives, you need to employ three types of lighting: ambient, task, and accent.

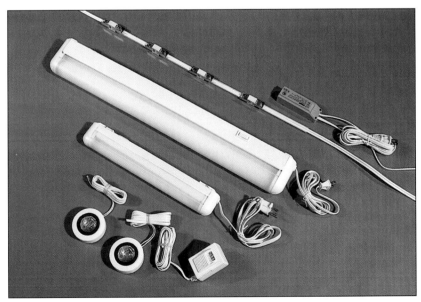

Halogen hockey pucks and accent strip lights are low-voltage fixtures. Shown in the center are two slim undercabinet fluorescents.

Fire-safety tips

The National Fire Protection Association offers the following advice on reducing the risk of a kitchen fire:

- Don't leave cooking unattended. Never leave the house while there's food cooking on the stove or in the oven.
- Keep the cooktop clean. Wipe up oil spills and spatters to prevent a grease fire.
- Don't overload electrical circuits. Plugging too many kitchen appliances into the same electrical outlet or circuit could cause the wires to overheat and catch fire.
- Dress appropriately. Garments with long, loose sleeves can catch fire if dangled too close to a hot stove burner.
- Clear clutter away from the cooktop. Keep all flammable objects – dish towels, curtains, pot holders, paper towels – well away from the stove.
- Inspect electrical cords. Never use an electrical appliance that has a cracked or frayed cord.

Fire extinguishers are classified according to the type of fire they can put out. Most kitchen extinguishers are rated B-C for fighting grease and electrical fires, although an A-B-C extinguisher is also suitable for kitchen fires.

Fire Safety

If you're wondering what fire safety has to do with remodeling a kitchen, consider this: The leading cause of all house fires is kitchen cooking appliances.

Smoke detectors

Smoke detectors form the first line of defense against a home fire. Building codes differ from town to town, but the national code stipulates that one smoke detector must be installed on every living level, including the basement. Many states also require a smoke detector in every bedroom.

However, smoke detectors aren't required for kitchens; in fact, they're not even recommended. That's because cooking smoke, fumes, and steam can trigger nuisance alarms which invariably lead people to disarm the detector (a big mistake).

Still, you can provide fire protection by installing a smoke detector just outside the kitchen, down the hall, or in an adjoining dining area.

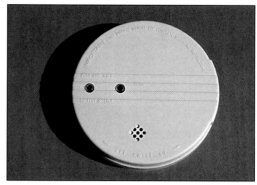

This smoke detector has two buttons: one for testing the battery and another for silencing nuisance alarms. The hush button allows you to override nuisance alarms by pressing a button. The detector automatically resets itself in about five minutes.

Smoke detectors are either battery powered or hardwired directly into the home's electrical system. Warning: Never wire a smoke detector into a circuit that's operated by a wall switch.

Fire extinguishers

Every kitchen should also be equipped with a portable fire extinguisher. But keep in mind, these units are only suitable for controlling small, contained fires. Before attempting to fight any home fire, get everyone out of the house and call the fire department.

Fire extinguishers are classified by the type of fire they can put out.
- Class A: Ordinary combustibles such as paper, wood, and cloth.
- Class B: Flammable liquids, like gasoline, grease, and oil.
- Class C: Electrical equipment, including appliances, wiring, circuit breakers, and fuse boxes.
- Multipurpose fire extinguishers, marked A-B-C, can be used to fight all three types of fires.

DEMOLITION

Make no mistake about it, demolition is dusty, dirty work that relies more on brute strength than careful calculation. However, there is a logical work sequence to follow to ensure that each step is done without injuring someone or wrecking the rest of the house.

A kitchen is dismantled in roughly the reverse order that it was originally installed. The first items to go are the appliances, followed by the plumbing fixtures, countertops, and cabinets.

If you've never tackled demolition work before, you'll probably be surprised at how fast it goes. Two people can reduce an average-size kitchen to a pile of rubble in about a day.

Prep

Before starting the actual demolition, move all small appliances, including the microwave oven, to the temporary kitchen. If there's a hanging light fixture, tie it up close to the ceiling to get it out of the way.

Empty the refrigerator before attempting to move it to a temporary location. If the unit has an automatic ice maker or water dispenser, don't forget to turn off the water before disconnecting the supply tube. Look for the shut-off valve under the sink, in the basement or crawl space, or behind the refrigerator.

To remove a dishwasher, first reach underneath the sink and close the shut-off valve that supplies hot water to the unit. If there isn't a shut-off valve, you will have to shut off the main valve. Then unplug the dishwasher and shut off the circuit that serves the dishwasher.

An appliance dolly is the safest and easiest way to move a refrigerator; it has a thick strap used to secure the appliance to the dolly. You can rent an appliance dolly for under $20.00 a day.

Disconnect the supply line and the drain hose by loosening the steel hose clamps. (Older dishwashers may have compression fittings instead of hose clamps.)

Pull off the dishwasher's lower front panel and disconnect the water supply tube and drain hose. If you can't pull the tube or hose free after loosening the hose clamps, simply cut them off with a utility knife.

Next, open the dishwasher door to see if the unit is fastened to the underside of the counter. You should see two small screws driven through metal tabs; remove them. Now grab the dishwasher near the bottom and slide it out from under the counter. If it seems jammed tight, try lowering the leveling legs. You may have to lift up slightly to clear the floorcovering.

If you're not planning to install a new kitchen floor, lay down a protective sheet of hardboard or thick cardboard before sliding out the dishwasher.

Open the dishwasher door and remove the mounting screws that are driven up into the underside of the counter.

Tape plastic over all heat registers, air-conditioning vents, and cold-air returns. Dust that gets in the cold-air returns will quickly be circulated all over the house.

To help contain dust in the work area, cover doorways to adjoining rooms with plastic. To allow access to the work area, overlap two sheets of plastic or install a zippered opening.

Plumbing Fixtures

The next step is to remove the sink. Begin by shutting off the main water supply to the kitchen. In most cases, that means temporarily turning off the water to the entire house. Look for the shutoff valve where the main water line enters the house; it's typically located next to the water meter or, if you have well water, near the pressurized storage tank.

Open the faucet to drain any remaining water and bleed out trapped air pressure. Next, use slip-joint pliers to loosen the trap nuts. If the sink is plumbed with PVC plastic fittings, you should be able to twist off the nuts by hand.

Then use a tubing cutter to cut the hot- and cold-water risers (those are the copper pipes connected to the faucet's flexible supply tubes). Leave about 4 inches of each pipe sticking up inside the cabinet.

Remove the sink next. Look up from inside the cabinet to see if there are metal clips securing the sink to the edge of the counter. Use a screwdriver to loosen the clips. If there aren't any clips, then the rim is probably just caulked to the countertop. Cut the caulk with a utility knife.

Push up on the bottom of the sink to free it from the counter. For a heavy enameled cast-iron sink, one of you will need to push up on one end while the other slips a wood block under the rim. Repeat for the other end. The blocks will provide space for your fingers so you can lift the sink out of the cabinet.

Finally, solder a copper cap onto each riser using a propane torch and lead-free solder. Then turn the water back on.

Disconnect the trap assembly and pull it free from the tailpiece. Place a small bucket under the trap to catch the water left in the trap.

Lift out the sink after removing any retaining clips from the underside of the counter. (Note that the faucet is still in place.)

Solder a copper cap onto each riser with a propane torch. Be careful of the open flame. First clear away all debris; a piece of scrap metal can be used to shield nearby wood.

Remove the doors, drawers, and loose shelves from the cabinets. If you're planning to reuse the cabinets, mark the cabinets, doors, and shelves so it's easy to match them up again later.

Counters and Cabinets

Most counters are held in place with screws driven up through corner blocks inside the cabinets. Back out all the screws, then pry the counter off the cabinets. If the backsplash is stuck to the wall, pry it off first. Place a shim between the prybar and the wall if you're planning to keep the walls.

Next, remove the cabinets, starting with the base units. First, figure out how the cabinets were attached to the walls. Some have screws driven into the wall through the horizontal rail at the upper rear of each cabinet. Remove these screws and any others driven through the face frames and into the adjoining cabinets. Older cabinets, especially site-built cabinets, are often attached with nails and will have to be pried away from the wall and floor.

Upper cabinets are mounted to the wall in much the same manner as the base cabinets. However, removing them is a two-person job: one to hold up the cabinet while the other loosens them from the wall. You may also find screws or nails driven straight up through the face frame or cabinet top and into a soffit or ceiling joist.

Island cabinets are usually fastened to blocking attached to the floor. First pry off any molding from around the base. Remove any screws you find behind the molding. If you find nails, drive them through with a drift punch. Then back out any screws that tie the cabinets together. If the cabinets won't budge, jam a long crow bar underneath and, using a 2x4 block as a fulcrum, pry the cabinets off the floor.

Back out *any screws driven through the face frames. On frameless cabinets you'll find the screws driven through the side panels.*

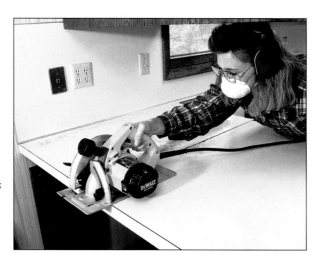

Cut *long countertops – especially L- or U-shaped counters – into smaller, easier-to-carry pieces.*

A prybar *makes quick work of removing older counters. With these, the plywood substrate was often nailed to the cabinet before the laminate was glued down.*

The cabinet should slide *right out once all the screws are removed. If it doesn't, tilt it forward or lift the front end and then slide it out.*

Walls and Ceilings

If your remodeling plans call for installing a new window (or enlarging an existing one), rerouting plumbing pipes, or upgrading the kitchen's electrical service, then you'll need to remove most of the old wall surface.

Don't use a saw to cut into the wall – you might sever a gas line, electrical wire, or plumbing pipe. Instead, pound a hole

Pry apart the soffit with a crow bar. Be ready to jump – there's a chance that once you start pulling it apart, the whole soffit will come crashing down.

The quickest way to take down drywall is to break it up with a 4-pound engineer's hammer.

through the drywall in the middle of a stud cavity. Then grab hold of the jagged edges of the drywall and pull to break off large pieces. Keep a trash can nearby for the drywall chunks. (Be sure to empty the can before it's full and too heavy to move.)

To tear down an old soffit, start by knocking a small hole through its side. Then peek in to see if the soffit houses any ducts, wires, or pipes. If it does, disconnect the mechanicals before demolishing the soffit.

Try to take the soffit apart in pieces, beginning with the bottom section. Use a sharp utility knife to score the seams both where the soffit meets the wall and ceiling, and along the front edge of the soffit. Pry the bottom free.

To remove the front section, work a prybar under the 2x2 that's attached to the ceiling. Work from inside the soffit in case the prybar damages the ceiling. That way any ceiling patches will be hidden by the new upper cabinets or soffit.

Pull off large chunks of drywall. Then use a claw hammer to yank the old nails from the studs.

Textured ceiling precautions

If your kitchen has a textured ceiling, it may contain asbestos. The good news is that asbestos poses no health risk unless it's friable (crumbly) and you inhale it. That's why it's important to never sand a textured ceiling.

To find out if your ceiling contains asbestos, scrape a few small samples into a plastic bag. Be sure to wear a respirator with HEPA (high efficiency particulate air) filters while you take the samples. Contact your state EPA office for the nearest asbestos testing laboratory.

If the samples test positive, the easiest remedy is to install new drywall over the ceiling. Or, call a licensed asbestos abatement company to remove the texturing or even the entire ceiling.

Flooring

It's usually best to cover the old floor with new underlayment, but that's not always practical. In some cases, the old floor is so badly damaged it must be ripped out. Or, the floor has been built up so much that adding another layer would create awkward transitions into adjacent rooms.

First, remove the baseboard and thresholds. For a wood floor, pry up the floorboards, starting at a threshold, using the longest pry bar you can find.

There's no easy way to remove a ceramic tile floor. Just get a big sledgehammer and start pounding away. Be sure to wear a dust mask, safety glasses, ear plugs, and gloves. Plow up the tile shards with a floor scraper.

Sheet vinyl flooring comes up easily if it's the perimeter-bonded type. Use a utility knife to slice through the flooring every 18 inches or so. Then simply pull up the unbonded strips.

If it's fully adhered vinyl, slice through it every 6 to 8 inches. Then wrap the end of a flooring strip around a cardboard core or a piece of PVC pipe. Roll the tube across the floor to peel up the flooring. Most of the felt backing will remain stuck down. To remove it, spray the felt with water and then scrape it up.

The best way to take up vinyl tiles is with an electric heat gun. Direct the hot air at the tile until the adhesive softens. Then lift the tile with a short-handled floor scraper.

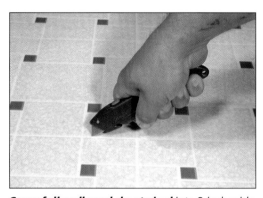

Score fully adhered sheet vinyl into 8-inch-wide strips. Pull up the strips of flooring, then scrape up the remaining backing and adhesive.

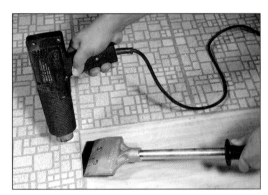

To remove vinyl tile, use an electric heat gun to warm the tiles and soften the adhesive below. Scrape up the tile a little at a time.

Asbestos alert

If your remodeling plans call for replacing an old resilient sheet or tile floor, the first step is to get a sample of the flooring tested for asbestos content. Resilient flooring, backing, and adhesive manufactured before 1982 are likely to contain some asbestos fibers.

To find a test lab, look in the phone book under "Laboratories, Analytical," or call your local health board or EPA office for a list of approved labs. The lab can tell you how big a sample is required, how to remove the sample safely, and how to package it.

If the test results turn up positive for asbestos you have a couple of options. When the flooring is in good shape, the most straight-forward solution is to leave the old flooring in place and put a new underlayment over top. Flooring that's in good condition poses no danger of releasing asbestos fibers.

If the old flooring is in bad shape (flaking or worn through), or if leaving it in place will cause the floor to be too high, the floor will have to be removed. Call a professional abatement company for this job. Breaking, cutting, or sanding the flooring and adhesive may release asbestos fibers into the air. Abatement professionals will take precautions to contain the fibers during the removal.

ROUGH-INS

The rough-in stage is the time to make necessary mechanical upgrades to your kitchen. The amount of rough-in work will depend upon the complexity of the new design. For example, if you're not planning to move the sink or add a second sink, there'll be few changes to the existing plumbing system. On the other hand, if you own an older house with badly corroded pipes, you may have to replumb the whole kitchen. And, if you plan to install an island, it may require new plumbing pipes, a gas line, electrical wiring, and a vent duct.

Replacing a Window

One decision you have to make about your replacement window is whether you want the new window to be bigger than the old one. Often, the window cannot be taller because the counter is in the way. If you widen the window, you will have to reroute any electrical cables or plumbing stacks located alongside the window.

Removing the old window

Start by prying the interior casing (molding), exterior trim, and siding from around the window. If possible, mark the new opening dimensions on the siding and cut it in place. You'll avoid problems with breakage, replacement, and paint matching if you do.

Then use a reciprocating saw fitted with a metal-cutting blade to cut any nails driven through the window's side jambs and into the jack studs. Be sure to wear safety goggles.

Next, working from the outside, use a prybar to pry the window free. If necessary, hold a 2x4 block against the interior edge of the jambs and pound the block with a hammer to loosen the window.

Hidden dangers

Fitted with the proper blade, a reciprocating saw will quickly slice through nearly any building material including gypsum, wood, metal, and plastic. You could easily sever a water pipe, gas line, or live electrical cable unless you're very careful when cutting into a wall, floor, or ceiling.

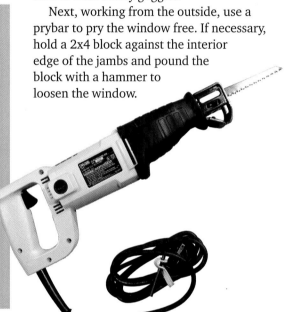

Enlarging the opening

The next step is to reframe the opening. First check whether the ceiling joists run perpendicular to the window wall. If they do, you must install a temporary 2x4 stud wall about 4 feet from the window wall to support the ceiling joists until the new header is in place.

Use a reciprocating saw and pry bar to remove the old sill, jack studs, king studs, and header from the opening. Also remove any wall studs that fall within the new, larger opening.

Remove entire lengths of siding only if you can't cut the siding in place. Handle the siding carefully and stack it safely out of the way so it can be reinstalled later.

After prying the window free, pass it through the opening (much safer than carrying it down a ladder). Large windows are easier to handle if you take out the sashes first.

Use a circular saw or reciprocating saw to cut back the sheathing. Set the blade depth of a circular saw so only the sheathing is cut, not the framing.

Now make a header that's 3 inches longer than the new window's rough-opening width. For a 2x4 stud wall, nail together two pieces of 2-by lumber separated by ½ inch plywood. For a 2x6 stud wall, fasten together two 2-by boards and then nail a 2x6 flat along the bottom edge of the header. (Check your local code about sizing the new header. If you're installing a bigger window, or if the code has changed since the house was built, you may need a beefier header than you had before.)

Cut two king studs and nail them to either end of the header. Cut two jack studs to fit under the header and extend down to the bottom, or sole, plate; nail those to the king studs. Stand the header assembly in the wall, center it on the window opening, and nail it in place. Then install a new sill and cripple studs.

Now cut back the sheathing to expose the new opening. Slip the window into position and check that it's plumb and level. Use shims to keep it in position, then nail through the exterior nailing flange with roofing nails. Nail wood windows through their brick mold with casing nails. Finally, install any exterior trim, and replace the siding.

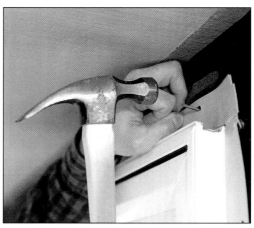

Installing a window takes two people: One outside to slip the window in place and later nail it into the framing (left), the other inside to check that the unit is level and plumb, and shim it into position (above).

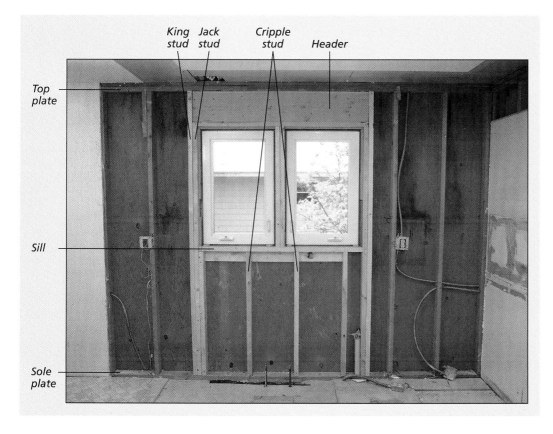

King stud   Jack stud   Cripple stud   Header

Top plate

Sill

Sole plate

The rough opening is generally about 1 inch wider and ½ inch taller than the window. The jack studs (also called trimmer studs) fit under the header, while the king studs extend up to the top plate.

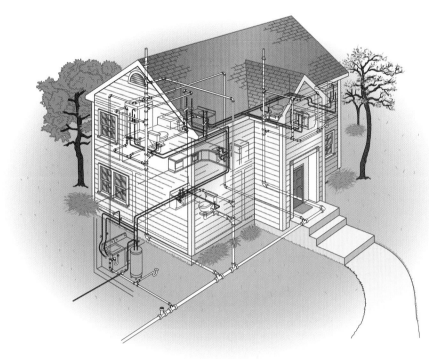

Your home's plumbing may seem like a complicated tangle of pipes, traps, drains, and vent stacks, but in reality is just two basic interrelated systems: 1) supply lines that deliver hot and cold water to the fixtures, and 2) drain-waste-vent (DWV) pipes that carry waste from the fixtures to the sewer or septic tank.

Plumbing Rough-Ins

A plumbing system is comprised of two sets of pipes: the supply system and the drain, waste, and vent (DWV) system. Plumbing codes are very specific about the size and type of pipes and fittings that must be used. To complicate matters, codes differ from state to state and from town to town. Be sure to check codes in your area before starting a plumbing project. Warning: Water and electricity are a potentially deadly duo. Before starting any rough-in work, turn off the water and electricity to the work area.

Drain pipe system

Start the rough-in work with the DWV system. It's easier to install these larger pipes before you run the smaller-diameter supply lines.

If you're putting the new sink in the same spot as the old one, simply reuse the old DWV pipes (assuming they're in sound condition). If you're planning to move the sink, check with your building department to see what's required.

1 *Scrape the inside edge* free of all burrs using a utility knife. Burrs left on the pipe will drag through the glue and weaken the bond.

2 *Apply PVC cleaner* to the inside of the fitting and also to the pipe end. The color makes it easy to find any spots you've missed.

Important

For proper drainage, be sure to slope the new sink's horizontal drain pipe at least ¼ inch per foot toward the vertical drain stack.

3 *Spread glue* onto the cleaned pipe and fitting – don't let it pool up in the fitting – and immediately join the parts.

4 *Push the pipe* all the way into the fitting, then give it a quarter turn. Hold the pipe in place for 10 seconds so the pipe doesn't pull out of the tapered fitting.

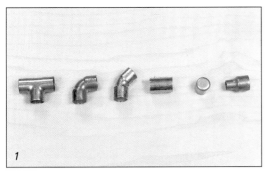

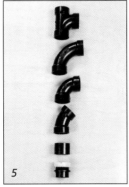

Plumbing parts. *Water-supply lines are almost always made of small-diameter copper tubing (1), although in homes built prior to World War II you might find threaded galvanized-steel water pipe (3). Some areas now allow CPVC tubing (2) for supply lines.*

PVC plastic (4) and ABS plastic (5) are code-approved nearly everywhere and commonly used for DWV systems. Parts used to assemble a sink trap (6) are connected with slip nuts.

Adding supply lines

Although there are four types of copper tubing, type M is the one commonly used for residential water-supply lines. Copper pipe is easily cut with a tubing cutter. The tubing lengths are connected with fittings and then soldered, or sweated, to form watertight joints. As with DWV pipe, you can extend old supply lines short distances.

1 *Clean the inside* of copper fittings with a wire brush. Flux will not adhere to a dirty surface, so be sure to buff off all grease, dirt, and oxidation.

2 *Clean the copper tubing* with a piece of abrasive emery cloth. Don't touch areas you've cleaned – fingerprints may impede the flow of solder.

3 *Apply flux* to the end of the pipe and to the inside of the fitting. Join the pipe and fitting and gently twist them back and forth to evenly spread the flux.

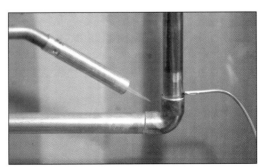

4 *Move the torch* back and forth to avoid burning off the flux. Heat only the fitting, never the pipe. Solder a cap onto each line.

Soldering tips

- Pipes that aren't absolutely dry won't heat up enough to melt solder. If all efforts to drain the pipe fail, stuff a piece of bread (white bread, no crust) in the pipe end. It will stop the moisture and eventually disintegrate.
- Once the solder starts to melt, pull the flame away from the fitting. The heat of the fitting will melt the solder.
- There's no need to move the solder around the joint. Capillary action will draw the solder into and around the joint.
- When the joint has cooled a minute, wipe it off with a wet rag. This will remove excess flux that would eventually corrode the copper.

To install a GFCI outlet, hook the wires coming from the service panel to the terminals marked LINE. Connect the outgoing wires to the terminals labeled LOAD. This adds GFCI protection to all the outlets that follow in the circuit.

Electrical Upgrades

Electrical rough-in work for a kitchen remodel typically includes adding or moving outlets and installing new light fixtures. For some upgrades, you'll be able to extend the existing electrical circuits, but for others, you'll have to add new circuits.

If your kitchen's electrical system hasn't been improved in the past 10 years or so, you'll likely have to upgrade it to meet the current electrical codes. For example, not long ago, the code stated that an outlet within 6 feet of a sink had to be protected by a ground-fault circuit interrupter (GFCI). Now all countertop outlets, regardless of their proximity to water, must offer GFCI protection.

Wiring basics

There are two basic ways to install new wiring. One approach is to tear out the drywall and insulation. This provides easy, unobstructed access for attaching the electrical boxes, boring holes, and running the cable; it is the most practical approach when installing several outlets and running several new circuits.

The second method is to bore holes from the basement up through the bottom wall plate and use a fish tape to pull new cable through the finished wall. You don't have to remove the drywall, but running the cable is a bit trickier.

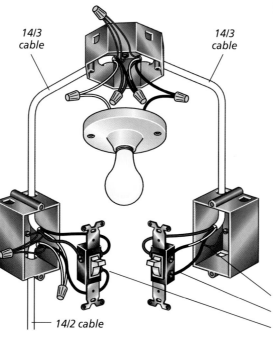

Three-way switches allow you to operate one fixture from two locations. One common way to make the connections is to bring power to one three-way switch with 14/2 cable, then run 14/3 cable to the light fixture and down to the second three-way switch.

14/3 cable

14/3 cable

14/2 cable

The electrical cable most commonly used in homes these days is nonmetallic-sheathed cable. A majority of the wiring will be done with either 14/2 or 12/2 cable. The first number refers to the gauge, or diameter, of the individual wires. (The lower the number,

1 *Mark the outline* of the electrical box on the wall. For retrofit situations, use a remodeling, or old work, box.

2 *Use a compass saw* or drywall utility saw to cut along the rectangular pencil outline of the electrical box.

White wire coded hot
Hot wire from fixture connects to common terminal
Hot wire from 14/2 supply cable connects to common terminal

the larger the wire.) The second number tells how many conducting wires there are in the cable. A grounding wire is also encased in the cable's plastic sheath. A three-way switch requires a 14/3 cable. High-amperage appliances, like a range, run off a hefty 6/3 cable.

Circuit considerations

As you plan electrical upgrades, keep in mind that each major kitchen appliance will require its own dedicated circuit. A microwave oven larger than 1,000 watts and a garbage disposer connected to a wall switch may also require dedicated circuits.

Two 20-amp circuits is the minimum requirement for countertop outlets. A range, cooktop, or wall oven will need a combination 120/240-volt, 50-amp outlet. If you're planning to install a gas range, don't forget that it'll need a 15-amp outlet to power its clock and electronic starter. Most refrigera-

Warning

For safety's sake, turn off the electricity to the entire kitchen before working on the electrical system. After you've connected a couple of new outlets and light fixtures, turn on the power only to those circuits (and only for work purposes).

3 **Bore** a ⅞-inch-diameter hole up through the subfloor and bottom plate of the kitchen wall.

5 **Use pliers to crimp** the cable onto the end of the tape. For insurance, wrap the connection with electrical tape so the cable doesn't come loose as you tug it up through the wall.

4 **Work the fish tape** down through the hole in the wall until it emerges in the basement. Be patient – it may take a few tries to get the fish tape through the hole.

tors operate off a 120-volt, 20-amp circuit. In some areas, the dishwasher and disposer can share a single 20-amp circuit.

Kitchen lights are usually on one 15-amp circuit. However, large kitchens with elaborate lighting schemes may need two circuits for the fixtures.

The electrical needs and code requirements for your kitchen may be different than those stated here; check with your local building department for specific requirements.

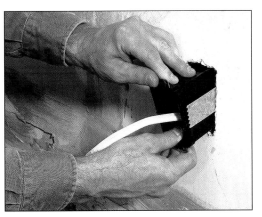

6 **Pull the cable** through the electrical box, then press the box into the hole until its metal tabs spring out and lock it in place.

It's very important to exhaust a vent to the outdoors. Try to plan as short and straight a duct run as possible.

If there's a soffit above the cabinets, you can run the ductwork into the soffit and out through an exterior wall.

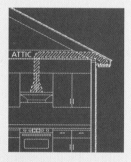

Another option is to extend the duct into the attic and then exhaust it out the soffit in the eave.

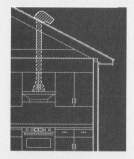

A third technique is to run the ductwork straight up into the attic and through the roof.

Island Rough-Ins

If your remodeling plans call for a center island, it'll probably require some rough-in work. How much work depends on how well-equipped the island is. For example, if it's going to house a gas cooktop and a sink, you'll need to rough-in a gas line, electrical cable, supply lines, DWV pipes, and ductwork for a vent hood or downdraft vent.

Even if the island is going to be devoted exclusively to storage and counter space it will require some rough-in work; code requires at least one outlet in an island.

There are two main concerns when roughing-in an island: Finding the most direct way to run the mechanical lines to the island, and making sure the lines come up through the floor in exactly the right spots. The last thing you want is a gas line poking up into the sink cabinet.

Running mechanical lines is usually a straightforward job, especially if your kitchen is over a basement. In most cases, you can simply tap into nearby water and drain lines and extend existing electrical circuits. An electric range or cooktop will require a new dedicated circuit run from the main electrical panel. Install the ductwork for a downdraft vent either between or under the floor joists.

Check with the local building department for the preferred way to run a gas line. The method you use will depend on several factors, including whether it's natural gas or bottled liquid propane (LP), and whether or not your home has an existing gas line.

Accurately locating each mechanical line, the second major concern, is easily accomplished by marking the positions of the cabinets on the floor. Use the actual cabinets as templates or take measurements off your scaled drawing. Once you know where the cabinets go, you can pinpoint where to drill or cut through the floor. Remember to check below for any obstructions.

After you've installed the rough-in lines, protect them by cordoning off the area with sawhorses and plywood. Place inverted buckets over protruding pipes and screw the buckets to the floor.

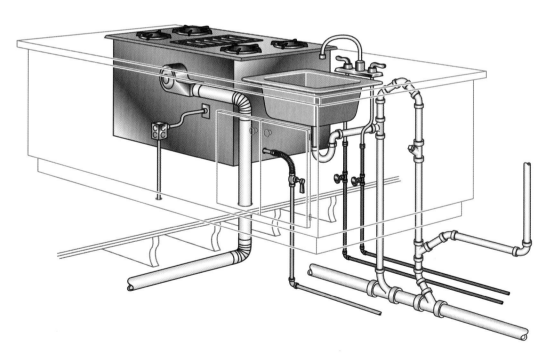

An island with a gas cooktop and a sink will need water lines, drain pipe, electrical cable, gas line, and vent ducting. The unusual piping behind the sink is a loop vent. With an island sink, code allows a loop vent that doubles over and runs under the floor to the nearest vertical stack. The horizontal vent pipe must be higher than the waste pipe and slope uphill so water doesn't get trapped in the loop.

Building a Soffit

A soffit is nothing more than a skeletal wood frame covered with ½-inch drywall. But, before building one, you must replace any drywall that's missing from the wall or ceiling. Most building codes don't allow soffits to be built over bare framing. That's because a fire that starts in a soffit could quickly travel through open stud cavities and spread throughout the house.

Layout

The first step in building a soffit is to snap chalk lines along the ceiling and wall to establish the placement of the 2x2 frame. Next, mark the locations of the ceiling joists and wall studs on the chalk lines. Then screw or nail a 2x2 to the line marked on the wall; be sure the fasteners go into the studs.

Framing

The front of the soffit frame resembles a ladder made of two 2x2s connected by 1x4 rungs. It's easiest to assemble the ladder frame on the floor and then install it as one piece. Cut a pair of 2x2s equal to the length of the soffit, then cut lengths of 1x4 equal to the soffit height, minus ½ inch for the drywall. Screw the 1x4s to the 2x2s, spacing them 24 inches on center.

Fasten this frame to the ceiling with screws driven up through the 2x2 and into the ceiling joists. Cut lengths of 1x4 to span the bottom of the soffit. Screw them to the 2x2 fastened to the back wall and to the front frame. Be sure each 1x4 butts against the wall and is flush with the outside edge of the frame. Install one every 24 inches.

Finishing

Finally, cover the soffit with ½ inch drywall. Install a metal corner bead along the front edge and finish all joints, including where the soffit meets the ceiling, with paper tape and joint compound.

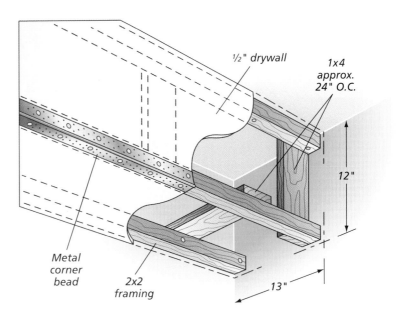

The main function of a kitchen soffit is to fill the open space between the top of the upper cabinets and the ceiling. It can also conceal plumbing pipes, steel beams, or ductwork that had to be roughed-in outside the walls or ceiling. A typical kitchen soffit is framed out of 2x2s and 1x4s, and then covered with ½-inch drywall.

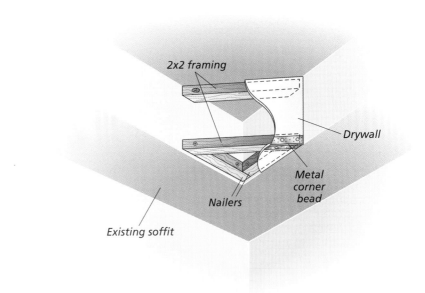

If you're replacing a blind corner cabinet with a diagonal-front corner cabinet, you may wish to build out the existing square-corner soffit to match the cabinet's angled face. Cut the ends of the front 2x2s to 45 degrees and screw them to the existing soffit framing. Additional 2x2s along the bottom edges serve as nailers for fastening drywall.

Repairing Drywall

To fix holes smaller than an inch in diameter, simply fill them with joint compound, or better yet, spackling compound (which shrinks less). Spread the compound with a 4- or 6-inch putty knife; let it dry completely. If necessary, apply more compound to level the holes. When the compound is dry, sand it flush with the wall.

For holes bigger than 12 inches, it's best to patch the hole. Remove the entire damaged section by cutting out the drywall from between two studs (or two joists, if working on the ceiling). Next, screw 1x3 cleats to the sides of the two exposed studs and to the drywall edges along the top and bottom of the enlarged hole. Let the horizontal cleats overhang into the hole by about an inch. Then cut a piece of drywall to fit into the hole and screw it to the cleats. Finish the patch with joint tape and joint compound.

Before installing any drywall, be sure the building inspector approves all the plumbing and electrical rough-in work. Then insulate the exterior walls. Insulation may also have to be inspected before it's covered with drywall.

1 *To repair holes up to 12 inches wide, install a drywall patch. Slip a wood strip into the hole and screw it in place. A screw driven into the strip provides a handle for holding it in place.*

2 *Position the drywall patch and drive screws up into the backing strip. For a good fit, cut the patch bigger than the hole. Hold the patch over the hole, mark its outline, then cut along the lines.*

3 *To conceal the patch, spread joint compound over the seams, then press in joint tape. Cover the patch with compound. Apply three coats, feathering each one to blend into the surrounding surface.*

CABINETS

You don't need any special skills *or innate abilities to install kitchen cabinets. What you do need is patience: rushing through this phase of the project can prove disastrous in the end.*

You'll also need your kitchen plan drawing which shows the size and placement of all the cabinets, filler strips, appliances, and other key components. Keep it handy and refer to it often to ensure that you're putting the right cabinet in the right place. There are dozens of parts and pieces and it's easy to get things mixed up if you don't pay close attention to the drawing.

Cabinet Layout

The first step of installing kitchen cabinets is marking level layout lines to help align the cabinets. The importance of this step cannot be overstated: The success of the entire installation relies on how accurately you mark the layout lines. If you make an error at this stage, it'll be compounded along the way and wreak havoc when it comes time to install the last cabinet, filler strips, and even the countertop.

Start the layout by finding the high spot in the floor. Place a 4-foot (or longer) level on the floor in front of each wall that'll have cabinets. If you don't have a long level, you can make one by placing a 2- or 3-foot level on top of a perfectly straight 8-foot 2x4. Use the level to find the highest spot on the floor, then mark it on the wall.

Next, measure up 34½ inches from the high spot and draw a level line onto the walls. This line represents the tops of the base cabinets without the countertop. Cabinets set on lower areas of the floor will be shimmed up to this line, creating a flush and level surface for the countertop.

Draw a second level line 19½ inches above the first. This line marks the bottom edge of the wall cabinets.

Now mark the center of each wall stud onto the two layout lines so you'll know where to drive the screws when you're hanging the cabinets.

Finally, check whether or not everything is going to fit. Mark the face frame width (not box width) of each cabinet on the walls. Also mark any open spaces where appliances will go. If you see a problem, take the time now to figure out a solution.

Customizing the layout lines

The line heights given here are pretty standard, but there are some situations in which you'll need to alter the heights.

If you will be laying a ceramic tile floor after the cabinets are installed, you need to add the height of the finish flooring and its underlayment to the height of the first level line. If you don't raise the base cabinets by the thickness of the flooring, you will bury a good portion of the cabinet toekick behind the flooring. It will also be difficult (if not impossible), to install undercounter appliances.

Placing the second layout line 19½ inches above the first allows for an 1½-inch-thick countertop plus an 18-inch space between the counter and the wall cabinets. If your plans call for something different, adjust the height of your second layout line accordingly.

1 *Use a long level* to find the highest spot on the floor. Check along every wall where cabinets will be installed. All the base cabinets will be shimmed up to this point to create a level run of cabinets.

2 *Measure up 19½ inches* from the first line to locate the bottom edge of the wall cabinets. This allows for an 1½-inch countertop and 18 inches between the counter and the wall cabinets.

3 *Draw a level line* around the room using the mark as a reference point. You will align the bottom edge of all the wall cabinets to this line.

4 *An electronic stud finder* offers a quick way to locate wall studs. If you use the old trial-and-error method of driving in a nail until you hit a stud, do it in an area that'll be hidden by the cabinets.

5 *A ledger supports* the wall cabinets while you install them. Screw a 1x2 or 1x3 to the wall, aligning it with the layout mark that represents the bottom edge of the wall cabinets. Once all the wall cabinets are installed, remove the ledger and fill any screw holes that won't be hidden by the backsplash.

Attaching the ledger

Prepare for installing the wall cabinets by attaching a temporary wood cleat, known as a ledger, to the wall. The ledger supports the weight of each cabinet as you jockey it into position.

Make the ledger from a long, straight 1x2 or 1x3. Hold it against the wall with its top edge flush with the upper layout line. Then fasten it with 2½-inch drywall screws driven into the wall studs.

Using a water level

A water level is one of the world's oldest, most accurate layout tools. It consists of nothing more than a clear plastic tube filled with water.

Start by making a single mark on one wall. For example, measure up 34½ inches to indicate the top of the base cabinets. Now, while one person holds one end of the tubing beside the reference mark, the second person carries the other end of the tube to another wall and slides it up or down until the water level at the first end aligns with the mark. When it does, mark the water level at the second end onto the wall. The two marks will be perfectly level with each other.

It takes only a few minutes to move the end of the tubing around the room and mark several reference points.

To make the level easier to read, put a few drops of food coloring into the water. Also, always tap out any bubbles from the tubing to avoid inaccurate readings.

Hanging Wall Cabinets

Before starting the installation, remove the cabinet doors and adjustable shelves and store them in a safe place. Put the hinge screws back into the mounting plates inside the cabinet for safekeeping. It's also a good idea to label and number each cabinet and all its parts so you can easily match them up later.

Corner cabinet

Begin the installation with a corner cabinet. Lift it into place and set it on top of the ledger. Hold the cabinet tightly against the walls, and check that its sides and face frame are perfectly plumb. It's likely that you'll have to slip shims behind one or both sides of the cabinet to make it plumb.

Before driving the screws, check for a gap between the wall and the hanging rail. If you find one, fill it with a shim wherever you plan to drive a screw. Otherwise, the screws will pull the hanging rail to the wall and knock the cabinet out of square.

Predrill the hanging rails, then drive 3-inch screws through the rails and into the wall studs. If the cabinet doesn't have hanging rails, simply drive the screws through the cabinet back and into the wall studs. Check that the cabinet is still plumb, then trim off excess shims sticking out from behind the cabinet.

1 *Install the corner* cabinet first. Take the time to get it perfectly plumb; any errors here will affect adjacent cabinets. Plus, the doors won't hang properly on a cabinet that isn't level, plumb, and square.

2 *Drive screws* through the hanging rails at the top and bottom of the cabinet and into a wall stud. (Predrill the rail to avoid splitting it.)

3 *Set the next cabinet* on the ledger beside the corner cabinet. Clamp the cabinets together, making sure the seam between the face frames is tight. If they're frameless cabinets, check for a tight seam where the two sides meet.

Plan ahead

If there's going to be an undercabinet light, bore a hole for the electrical cable through the bottom, rear flange before installing the cabinet.

Adjacent cabinets

Once the corner unit is installed, set the next cabinet in place and clamp the two together. Be sure the face frames align perfectly.

Next, use a combination bit to bore three pilot holes through the edge of one vertical face frame (called the stile) and into the other. Fasten the face frames together with 2½-inch screws.

To fasten frameless cabinets together, bore three holes completely through the sides, about 2 inches back from the front edges. Then join the two cabinets with the special fasteners provided by the manufacturer. If none were furnished, buy either binding screws (a two-part, male/female threaded fastener) or machine screws with cap nuts.

Press the opposite end of the cabinet against the wall and check its side and face frame for plumb. Insert shims where needed and then drive screws through the hanging rails and into the wall studs. Continue installing cabinets in this manner along one entire wall. Then move back to the corner and start working out the other direction.

4 *Bore through the stile* of one face frame and partway into the other with a combination bit. This bit cuts both the pilot hole and the countersink.

5 *Fasten the face frames* together with drywall screws. The pilot holes will prevent the screws from splitting the wood. (Note that the screw is located so it will be hidden by the hinge plate.)

6 *To position* short cabinets that won't rest on the ledger, measure up from the ledger to locate the cabinet top and extend a level line out from the adjacent cabinet tops.

7 *Clamp* the short cabinet to the adjacent cabinet and level it across the top. Check the face frame and end for plumb, shim as needed, then screw the cabinet to the wall.

Base Cabinets

Base cabinets are installed in roughly the same order as wall cabinets; you start with the corner unit – usually a large carousel cabinet or a standard cabinet and a blind corner cabinet meeting at a right angle – then work out along each wall. However, base cabinets are often a bit more difficult to set perfectly level and plumb because they're affected by the conditions of both the floor and wall.

Blind corners

If you're putting in a blind cabinet, check the plan drawing to see if there's a filler strip that goes between the blind cabinet and its neighbor (there usually is). The filler strip puts some space between the cabinets so the opposing doors and drawers can open without slamming into each other.

Start the installation by shimming the blind cabinet plumb and level. Next attach the filler strip to the second cabinet by driving 2½-inch drywall screws through the stile and into the filler strip. Set the second cabinet in place, shimming it plumb and level. Drive screws through the blind cabinet's stile into the edge of the filler strip.

Carousel corners

Carousel units with full backs are installed pretty much like other angled wall cabinets. Installing a backless carousel is a bit more complicated. With these, you start by fastening 1x3 cleats to the two walls behind the unit to support the countertop. Be sure the top edges of the cleats are aligned to the 34½-inch layout line.

The rounded back of the carousel cabinet also makes it difficult to position the unit

1 **Fasten a backless corner** *carousel to the adjacent cabinets. Align the assembly with the wall cabinets above, shim it level and plumb, and attach it to the wall. (Note the rear, corner cleats that will support the counter.)*

2 **Insert shims** *under each cabinet to raise it up to the layout line marked 34½ inches above the highest spot on the floor.*

Compensating for a slanted floor

In extreme cases, where the floor is out of level by ¾ inch or more, it's not practical to shim the cabinets to the layout line. Instead, screw 2½-inch-wide plywood strips to the floor. Put down two parallel strips to support the front and rear edges of all the cabinets located in the low area. Then you'll only need very thin shims to raise the cabinets to the layout line. Be aware you may need bigger base trim to hide the blocking.

3 *Fasten base cabinets* by driving screws through the hanging rail into a wall stud. Use thin shims to fill gaps between the rail and the wall. Otherwise, as the screw is tightened, it will twist the cabinet and distort the face frame.

exactly square in the corner. For that reason, set the adjacent square cabinet first. Shim the cabinet up to the layout line. Then check it for plumb along its sides and face frame, and for level across its top from side-to-side and front-to-back. Insert shims where necessary to adjust the cabinet – but don't screw it in place just yet.

Next, set the carousel cabinet into position and shim it level and plumb. Align the two cabinets and fasten them together with screws driven through the face frames. Install the cabinet on the other side of the carousel cabinet in a similar manner. At this point, you'll have three cabinets joined together to form one large L-shaped assembly. Check that the assembly is square. If necessary, slip shims behind the rear of the two end cabinets to square up the corner assembly.

Installing the corner unit

The corner cabinets are now ready to be screwed to the wall studs. But before you do that, check one more time that everything is level, plumb, and square. Slip shims into any gaps between the drywall and the hanging rails. Screw the cabinets to the wall, making sure to drive the screws into studs.

Continue installing the base cabinets out from the corner along one wall, then start on the other.

When you come to a spot where an appliance will be installed, leave an opening to the exact width specified by the manufacturer.

4 *After shimming the cabinets* to be level and plumb, clamp together the face frames. Make sure the faces are perfectly aligned before boring pilot holes and driving in screws.

Cutouts for plumbing and electrical fixtures

Before setting the sink cabinet, bore holes for the water-supply lines and drain pipe. Use a 1-inch-diameter spade bit to bore holes for the supply pipes and a hole saw to cut the hole for the drain line.

Use a jig saw to cut openings in the cabinet back for any electrical outlets. A hole drilled at the corner of the cutout provides a starting point for the jig saw blade.

Filler Strips

Any gaps between the walls and the end cabinets are hidden by boards called filler strips. The strips come prefinished to match the cabinets and are wider than needed so you can scribe them to fit exactly.

Start by clamping the strip to the cabinet's face frame. Don't worry about any gaps or uneven spaces along the wall, just make sure that the stile and filler strip are perfectly parallel.

Next, spread a compass to the width the filler strip overlaps the cabinet face frame. Then slide the compass with its metal pivot point riding along the wall and its pencil tip marking the filler strip. Any irregularity or unevenness in the wall will be transferred to the strip.

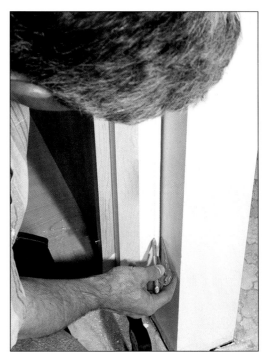

1 *Use a compass* to scribe the filler strip to the wall. Put masking tape on the filler strip so your pencil line will be clearly visible.

Unclamp the filler strip and use a jig saw or circular saw to rip it close to the pencil line. Use a belt sander to sand off the remaining waste wood down to the line. Test fit the filler strip. If it's still too tight, sand a little more and try again. Once you're satisfied with the fit, fasten the filler strip by screwing through the face frame stile.

Instead of separate filler strips, custom cabinets often have extended stiles. On these units, the stiles on the end cabinets are made extra wide to overhang the cabinet edge by a few inches. You scribe the stile to fit the wall, just as you would a filler strip.

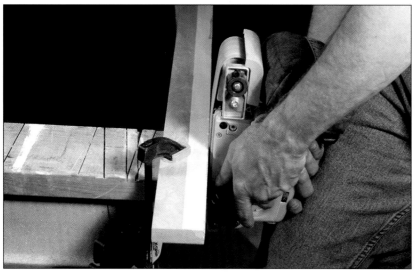

2 *Saw off* most of the waste, then use a belt sander to sand down to the pencil line. Lean the sander back slightly to undercut the edge of the filler strip.

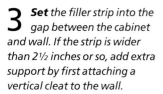

3 *Set* the filler strip into the gap between the cabinet and wall. If the strip is wider than 2½ inches or so, add extra support by first attaching a vertical cleat to the wall.

4 *Secure the strip* with screws driven through the stile. If there's a cleat, face-nail the filler strip to the cleat with 4-penny finishing nails. Be sure to prebore pilot holes. Set the nails and fill the holes with a putty stick.

Decorative Trim

Most cabinet manufacturers now offer a wide array of prefinished accessories, including crown moldings, dentil strips, valances, soffit moldings, interior corner strips, and undercabinet trim. The accessories provide an easy way to add style and architectural interest to stock cabinets.

Cut the trim to length with a power miter saw or a miter box and backsaw. Fasten the pieces with finishing nails, but be sure to pre-bore pilot holes to avoid splitting the wood. If you don't have the correct size drill bit to bore pilot holes, try this trick: Chuck a finishing nail into the drill and use it to bore perfect-sized pilot holes. Apply only light pressure to the drill to avoid bending the thin-shank nail.

Predrill pilot holes when nailing up crown molding or other decorative trim. If you don't, the nails will split the molding.

Stock cabinets, custom look

You can easily create a custom look with stock cabinets, all you need is a little imagination and the courage to break the rules.

Stock cabinets come in dozens of widths, but in only a handful of different depths and heights. However, by mixing and matching the cabinets available (which can include bath vanities from the same cabinet line), and ordering extra shelves and finished panels, you can produce a one-of-a-kind kitchen.

For example, the baking center shown at left was made by placing a butcherblock counter on a bath vanity base cabinet. The vanity is 3 inches shorter and 3 inches shallower than the kitchen base cabinets, so it looks custom made.

In the photo shown above, a short wall cabinet that's typically used over a refrigerator was aligned with the bottom of the wall cabinets to create an open-shelf storage niche. The window seat was made by setting a short wall cabinet on a toekick.

Island Cabinets

Many of the techniques used to install base cabinets are also employed when building a center work island. The major differences are that island cabinets are fastened to the floor (instead of the walls), and the backs of the cabinets must be concealed.

Installing the cabinets

After marking the location of the island on the floor, temporarily set the cabinets into place. Draw an outline around each cabinet, then move it out of the way. Now make another set of marks to represent the inside dimension of the cabinets. Measure in from each outline by the thickness of the cabinet's sides, toekick, and back.

Next, cut a pair of 2x2 cleats for each end cabinet; the cleats will run along the cabinet sides. Lay the cleats flush with the inner lines and fasten them to the floor with 3-inch drywall screws. Set the cabinets into place over the cleats. Shim the cabinets as needed so they are level and plumb. Then drive 4-penny (1½-inch) finishing nails through the side of the cabinets and into the cleats.

Now install one cleat to anchor the back of each mid-run cabinet. To attach these units, screw through the face frames and nail into the cleat.

Hiding the cabinet backs

Conceal the exposed backs of the island cabinets with a plywood panel. If prefinished panels aren't available from the cabinet manufacturer, make your own from ¾-inch-thick, furniture-grade plywood. Since face frames extend past the cabinet fronts, the panel

1 *Mark* the location of the island on the floor using your kitchen plan for reference. Remember that aisle widths are measured counter edge to counter edge; be sure to account for toekick spaces and counter overhang when plotting the island placement.

3 *Position the 2x2 cleats* for the end cabinets so they will fit tight against the inside edges of the cabinets. Fasten the cleats with 3-inch screws.

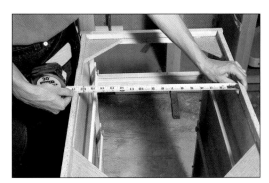

2 *Set the cabinets temporarily* in place. Mark the outline of each cabinet on the floor. Measure the inside width of each island cabinet to determine the placement of the wood cleats.

4 *Slowly lower* an end cabinet over the 2x2 cleats. The cabinet should fit snugly against the cleats. If it doesn't, reposition the cleats.

5 *Align the tops* of the end cabinets with a long level. Slip shims underneath to adjust the cabinets perfectly level and plumb.

6 *Secure the cabinets* by nailing or screwing through the sides and into the 2x2 cleats. Position the fasteners low so the heads will be hidden by the base trim.

should extend past the side of each end cabinet the same amount, usually about ³⁄₁₆ inch. Conceal the exposed ends of the plywood panel with a solid-wood end strip that's the same size as the face frame stile (typically 1½ inch wide).

To determine the length of the plywood panel, measure across the two end cabinets, subtract 2⁵⁄₈ inch from your reading and cut the plywood to that dimension. Next, attach the 1½-inch-wide end strips using biscuit splines or dowel pins. Stain and finish the panel to match the cabinets, then fasten it with glue and finishing nails.

7 *Conceal* the back of the cabinets with a panel made of furniture-grade plywood. The edges of the plywood are concealed with wood strips cut to the same width as the face frame stiles on the cabinets.

8 *Hold the panel* in place with bar clamps, then secure it with finishing nails driven near the bottom and top of each cabinet.

Top view

Existing joists

Blocking assembly

½" x 5½" x 7½" plywood flange

2x6 blocking

3" drywall screw

Ceiling

Cabinet

Filler piece

Side view

I-beam blocks fastened between joists provide solid support for ceiling-mounted cabinets that run parallel with the joists. To hang the cabinet, screw through the cabinet and up into the 2x6 blocking.

Ceiling-Mounted Cabinets

Most cabinet companies make cabinets that are specifically designed for mounting to the ceiling above a peninsula counter. They're called double-faced cabinets when they have doors on both sides.

If the cabinets run perpendicular to the ceiling joists, the installation is pretty straightforward. Mark the centerline of each joist onto the ceiling. Get two people to hold the cabinet in position while you fasten it with 3- or 4-inch screws (and washers) driven through the cabinet top and into the joists.

The installation is a little more complicated when the cabinets are parallel with the joists. One option for supporting the cabinets is to toenail blocking between the joists, but I-beam blocking is stronger, as well as easier to install.

To make an I-beam block, screw ½-inch plywood flanges onto a 2x6. Spread glue onto the flanges, slip the block into the ceiling and screw it to the joists. After patching the drywall, hoist the cabinet into position and drive screws with washers through the cabinet top into the blocking.

This peninsula cabinet is screwed to the ceiling joists and trimmed with crown molding. Unless the placement is carefully planned, ceiling-hung cabinets can block light and sightlines from one part of the kitchen to the other. Glass-panel doors help keep the cabinet from blocking light.

These double-faced cabinets have glass-panel doors on both sides. The open area below serves as a convenient pass-through space from the kitchen to the dining room.

Refacing Cabinets

Refacing consists of covering the old face frames and exposed ends of the cabinets with new wood or plastic laminate, and installing replacement doors and drawer faces. This is much quicker and less expensive than installing new cabinets, but consider it only if you're content with the kitchen's present layout.

To save money on a refacing job, you can order the materials from a cabinet refacing company, then do the installation work yourself. Someone from the refacing company will come out to measure the cabinets and show you a catalog of various door and drawer styles. After placing the order, expect to wait at least two or three weeks for the parts to be delivered.

Face frames first

Begin by covering exposed ends of cabinets with a thin plywood filler piece to bring the surface flush with the face frame edges. Next, cut a piece of ¼-inch finished plywood slightly larger than the end of the cabinet. Attach the finished panel to the filler piece, then use a router with a flush-trimming bit to cut away the excess plywood.

Now cut the pieces that will cover up the stiles and rails of the face frame. Depending on the refacing company, the pieces might be ¼-inch- or ⅜-inch-thick solid-wood sheets, wood veneer, or plastic laminate. Apply wood veneer and plastic laminate with contact cement. Use carpenter's glue and pin nails (brads) to secure solid-wood stock.

1 ***The most economical way*** *to reface cabinets is to order new doors, drawer fronts, and facing materials from a refacing company and do the installation yourself. Before the new parts arrive, remove all the old doors and drawers. This is also a good time to clean and paint the shelves.*

2 ***Measure*** *the cabinet end, then cut a piece of plywood filler to bring the side flush with the face frame.*

3 ***Spread glue*** *onto the filler piece and nail it to the cabinet with pin nails. Then cut a piece of finished plywood to cover the entire end.*

4 ***Apply carpenter's glue*** *to the finished plywood panel, press it against the cabinet end, and secure it with pin nails.*

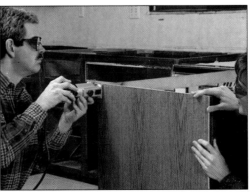

5 ***Trim off the excess*** *plywood using a router and a flush-trimming bit; a ball-bearing pilot rolls along the face frame to control the cut. Then sand the plywood edges smooth.*

6 **Cover** *the face frame with plastic laminate, veneer, or prefinished wood stock. Carefully cut a piece to fit each rail and stile.*

Installing doors and drawers

Mark hinge locations on the stiles and the doors; using a wood block as a marking template makes this process faster and more accurate. Fasten the hinges to the doors, hold the doors in position, and tighten the mounting screws.

If the drawers have a drawer front with an attached drawer face, simply unscrew the old drawer face and attach the new one.

If the drawers have one-piece, integral drawer faces, you must create drawer fronts of ½-inch plywood. Glue and nail them between the drawer sides. Now glue and screw the new drawer faces to the plywood fronts.

7 **A pneumatic pin nailer** *provides a quick, easy way to attach thin stock. You could also use a hammer and small brads.*

8 **Don't forget** *the toekick. After refacing the face frame of the cabinets, glue and nail finished stock to the toekick.*

9 **Fasten one side** *of the hinge to the inside of the door. Space the hinges 3 inches from the top and bottom edges of the door.*

10 **Secure the door** *to the cabinet with hinge-mounting screws. Use a wood block as a template for marking the stiles. Install a pair of doors, then adjust them for even spacing.*

11 **Glue and clamp** *the new drawer face to the drawer. Before attaching it, install the drawer to see if the face is properly aligned.*

COUNTERTOPS

With the cabinets in place, it's time to tackle the countertops. How much of the work you do yourself will depend mostly on the type of countertop you've chosen. For example, fabricating a solid-surface or granite counter should be left to a professional.

However, if your plans call for a plastic-laminate or ceramic tile counter, there's plenty you can do. With either of those materials, you'll be able to invest as much sweat equity as you'd like into the design, construction, and installation of the counter.

Plastic-Laminate Counters

The best place to fabricate a laminate countertop is a large, well-ventilated work area. To avoid getting debris in the contact cement, the work area should be as clean and dust-free as possible. If the countertop sections are small and maneuverable, try to work outside or in a garage. Large, angled countertops are best built right in the kitchen.

Building the substrate

Laminate countertops only look as if they're 1½ inches thick. In reality, the countertop is one layer of ¾-inch particleboard with an extra strip of particleboard attached at the front. The front build-up strip rests on the front edge of the cabinets. Strips of particleboard are glued and nailed to the cabinet tops to support the rest of the countertop.

Cutting plastic laminate

The technique for cutting plastic laminate will vary depending on the type of saw you use. For a portable circular saw, lay the laminate face down onto a sheet of particleboard supported on 2x4s. Be sure to sweep the particle-board clean of any sand or grit before laying down the laminate.

Always mark the laminate at least an inch wider and longer than needed – you'll rout off the excess later. Use a straightedge to mark the cut lines on the laminate. For long cuts, snap chalk lines.

Attaching the edge strips

When you attach the edge strips, do the end pieces first, then the front. That way, you won't be able to see the corner seams when you're standing in front of the counter.

Use an inexpensive paint brush to apply an even coat of contact cement to the back of the strips. Check to make sure you didn't miss any areas. If you've got several laminate strips, lay them side by side and use a glue

1 *Reinforce* seams in the particleboard substrate. Usually, a 12-inch-wide gusset is used to join the sections and reinforce the joint. This gets glued and screwed to the underside of the particleboard.

2 *Build up the front edge* of the counter to 1½ inches thick by attaching a 4-inch-wide strip of particleboard. Use glue and 1¼-inch drywall screws to attach the strip.

3 *Glue and nail* particleboard strips to the top edges of the cabinets; these will support the counter. (Note that a strip is also placed along the back edges of the cabinets, parallel with the wall.)

4 *Support plastic laminate* on particleboard to prevent it from cracking when you cut it with a circular saw. Set the blade no more than ½ inch deep. To avoid chipping the laminate, place it face down.

roller to coat them all at the same time.

Next, brush cement onto the edge of the counter, wait a few minutes, then apply a second coat. The extra cement is needed because the porous edge of the particleboard will soak up most of the first coat.

When the cement feels tacky you can attach the laminate strips. Remember, it's called contact cement because it bonds on contact; the instant the two surfaces touch together, they become stuck. Make sure the strip is positioned so it will extend past all four sides of the countertop face before touching the strip against the edge.

Allow the cement to set up before trimming the excess. Rout off the excess laminate with a flush-trimming bit. Finally, use a belt sander or laminate file to smooth the laminate edge perfectly flush with the counter.

5 *A table saw* is ideal for cutting narrow strips of laminate for backsplashes and edges. To avoid chipping, cut the laminate face up. A board clamped to the rip fence keeps the laminate from sliding underneath.

6 *Use an inexpensive* 3-inch-wide paint brush to apply a thin, even coat of contact cement to the back sides of the laminate strips and to the edge of the particleboard substrate.

7 *Wait for the contact cement* to become tacky (usually 10 minutes or longer). Contact cement bonds instantly so position the strip carefully before pressing it onto the edge.

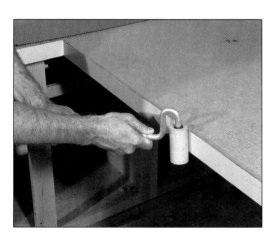

8 *Use a J-roller* to firmly press the edge strip into the contact cement and to remove air pockets. Run the roller back and forth several times along the entire length of the laminate strip.

9 *Trim off the excess* laminate from the front-edge strip using a laminate router (shown here) or a router fitted with a ball-bearing piloted, flush-trimming bit.

Which way to run a router

Generally speaking, it's best to run a router from left to right when standing with the router between you and the piece of work. Router bits rotate clockwise. When the router is moved left to right the bit pulls the router into the work, resulting in a clean, close cut. If you move the router right to left, the bit pushes away from the work. This can make for a wavy cut, and the router could even take off on you.

Appearances can be deceiving, though. Put the work between you and the router, and you need to run the router right to left. If in doubt, remember that you'll feel resistance when moving the router in the correct direction.

11 *Stickers keep the laminate* from bonding to the substrate while you position the laminate. Use wood dowels, plywood strips, cardboard or, our favorite, slats salvaged from an old vinyl mini-blind.

10 *Pour* contact cement onto the back of the laminate and spread it evenly with a 9-inch-wide glue roller. Coat the particleboard the same way. Let the contact cement dry until it is tacky (usually 10 minutes or longer).

Applying laminate to the countertop

The easiest way to apply large amounts of adhesive is to dump it right out of the can. Use a glue roller to spread the contact cement over the substrate and the back of the laminate. (These disposable rollers won't shed fibers into the contact cement like a paint roller will.) If you can't find a glue roller, use a paint roller with the shortest nap you can find.

The glued surfaces will bond instantly. To give you time to position the laminate, lay narrow strips (called stickers) across the substrate. Then shift the laminate into position, making sure it overhangs the substrate on all edges. When you're sure the laminate is in the right position, pull out the stickers one at a time, starting in the middle of the counter. After you've removed a few, press down on the laminate to adhere it to the substrate. Continue working this way toward each end of the counter.

Use a J-roller to roll the laminate into the contact cement. Work from the middle out to the edges. Be very careful when working near the edges. If the roller veers off the laminate while under pressure, it'll crack the edge that overhangs the counter.

Trim off the excess laminate with a laminate router or a router with a flush-trimming laminate bit. (This has a ball-bearing pilot to help guide the router.) Clean and lubricate the bearing to keep it spinning freely; the bearing might seize up and burn a streak into the laminate if it gets clogged with contact

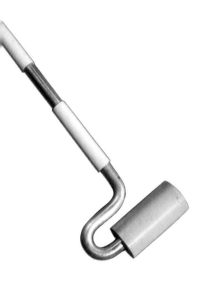

12 *Pull the stickers out* one at a time, starting in the middle. After pulling out a few stickers, start pressing the laminate into the contact cement. If there's a seam, apply contact cement to the entire substrate, but bond the laminate pieces one at a time.

13 *Use a J-roller* to press down the laminate and permanently set it into the contact cement after all the stickers are removed. Roll back and forth across the entire surface several times, working in all directions.

cement and laminate shavings.

After routing off the excess, the top laminate piece will overhang the front-edge laminate by a just a hair. Remove the overhang with a laminate file. Hold the file at about 60 degrees to the top surface and stroke downward until you see a bead of contact cement break away from the seam; then hold the file at 45 degrees and use long strokes to ease the sharp corner.

14 *Remove the overhanging* laminate with a router. The flush-trimming bit shown here has a ball-bearing pilot that rolls along the front edge of the counter, giving greater control over the cut.

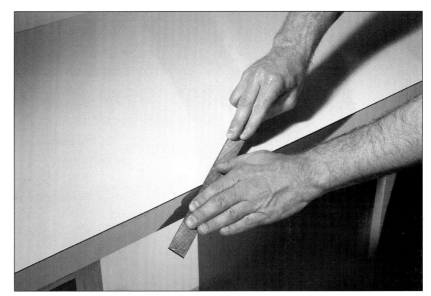

15 *Trim and smooth* the edge with a laminate file. Make two passes. On the first, make downward strokes with the file held at a 60-degree angle. Then ease the edge with the file held at about 45 degrees.

Eye-catching edges

Add pizzazz to your plastic-laminate counter by creating a decorative edge treatment. Two that are easy to do are hardwood bevels and pinstriping. In both cases, the key steps are done before attaching the laminate to the edges and top surface.

Hardwood bevel

To create a hardwood-bevel edge, start by fastening a ⅜-inch-thick by 1½-inch-wide hardwood strip to the edges of the particleboard substrate with carpenter's glue and finishing nails. Cut miter joints where two strips meet at an outside corner. Next, apply laminate to the edges and top surface, covering up the hardwood strip. Then rout a 45-degree bevel in the counter's edge to expose the hardwood.

Pinstripe

To produce a pinstriped edge, cement two or three different colored laminate strips to the edges of the substrate, then laminate and trim the top surface. Next, bevel the edge with a chamfering bit to reveal the pinstripes. Note that this technique only works with color-through laminate, the kind that has the surface color running all the way through the sheet.

Hardwood bevel

Pinstripe

Counter installation

It doesn't take very long to install a kitchen counter, but it does require at least two people to carefully set it into place; to handle a large U-shaped counter, get three people.

Before setting the counter onto the cabinets, lay a bead of adhesive caulk along the particleboard support strips nailed on the cabinets. Slide the counter in at an angle with one end lifted in the air, then push down on the raised end. For an L- or U-shaped counter, set the longest section and raise the shorter portion. Secure the counter by driving screws up through the corner blocks inside the cabinets.

Backsplash basics

After screwing the counter to the cabinets, fabricate the backsplash using the same techniques you used to make the counter. Scribe the backsplash to match any irregularities in the wall. Make the backsplash out of ½- or ¾-inch-thick particleboard ripped about 4 to 6 inches wide. Also rip some strips no more than ¼ inch thick. Glue these to the substrate to create a scribing strip. The strips should be flush to the top and exposed ends.

Apply plastic-laminate strips to both the top and bottom edges, then to the face. (The bottom strip protects the particleboard from wicking up the water that'll inevitably seep between the counter and backsplash.)

16 *Drive screws* up through the corner blocks to attach the counter. The length of screw required depends on the distance from the corner block to the countertop. Make sure the screws you use aren't too long.

17 *Apply plastic laminate* to the face of the particleboard backsplash after attaching laminate strips to the edges. The application order is important if you want the seams to be hidden.

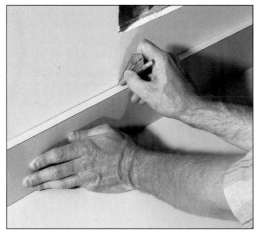

18 *Use a compass* to transfer any wall irregularities onto the backsplash. Then sand the backsplash to fit.

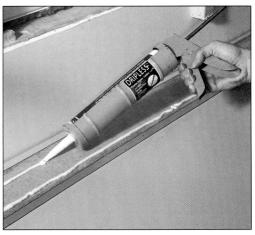

19 *Lay two parallel* beads of adhesive caulk onto the rear of the backsplash; run another bead along the counter.

Depending on how much of the scribe strip remains after sanding it down, you may need to glue shims to the back of the backsplash along the bottom edge so it will lay flat against the wall. Fasten the backsplash to the wall with adhesive. Run a bead of caulk where the backsplash meets the counter and another where it meets the wall.

20 **Brace the backsplash** *until the adhesive dries. Use clamps, 2x4 blocks, braces made from scrap lumber, and shims to press the backsplash down and drive it flat to the wall.*

Counters for islands

Building and installing island counters isn't much different than building any other counter, except for two details.

First, any overhang greater than 12 inches will require support brackets. Position the braces every 18 to 24 inches, as necessary.

Second, an island countertop is exposed on all sides and frequently has curves instead of corners. In this situation, it's much easier to simply double up the entire substrate than to mess with 4-inch-wide build-up strips. Just remember that you don't attach any support strips to the cabinet tops when you use this method.

Install braces to support counters that overhang the cabinets by more than 12 inches. Attach wooden braces by driving screws into the braces from inside the cabinet. Metal braces are usually screwed directly to the outside of the cabinet.

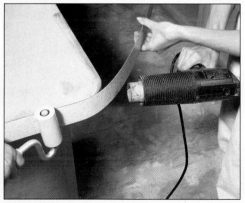

Use a heat gun to ease laminate around tight curves. Slowly bend the strip as it heats up, then press it into the contact cement with a J-roller.

After adhering laminate to the top of the particleboard substrate, use a router fitted with a flush-trimming bit to cut off the excess laminate. Then file the joint smooth.

Making a sink cutout

If your sink came with a template, it will include directions telling exactly where to position it on the counter. If there is no template, check that the sink cutout you draw is centered over the sink cabinet and perfectly parallel with the front edge of the counter. It must also be far enough back from the front edge so the sink bowl will clear the cabinet face frame when it's dropped into place.

Before drawing the lines, mark the rough outline onto the counter with masking tape strips. The masking tape will make your pencil lines easier to see and will also keep the saw from chipping the laminate.

Now trace the cutout onto the masking tape. If a template isn't available, use a framing square to mark the basic form and a compass to scribe an arc at each corner.

1 *If you don't have a template*, check the installation instructions for the dimensions of the sink cutout, or take measurements right off the sink. Put down strips of 2-inch-wide masking tape and use a framing square to mark the outline of the sink cutout. Make sure that the cutout is centered over the sink cabinet.

2 *Use a compass* to trace an arc at each corner. Also trace the arc onto a piece of cardboard, cut it out, and test-fit it to the sink bowl.

3 *Make the straight cuts* with a circular saw. Start by making the two cuts at the left and right sides of the cutout. Then make the two straight cuts along the front and rear of the cutout. You could use a jig saw for the whole cutout, but cutting straight is easier with a circular saw.

4 *Cut along the curves* with a jig saw. The support board that's screwed to the sink cutout will prevent the waste piece from falling down inside the cabinet. Lift out the waste piece and test-fit the sink.

Postformed Counters

You can special-order a postformed laminate counter to an exact length, but if you buy one off the rack, you'll have to cut it to fit. The best way to trim a postformed counter is to turn it upside down and cut from the backside. A circular saw will produce a clean straight cut, but it can't slice all the way through the backsplash – you'll have to finish up with a handsaw or jig saw. Since laminate tends to chip when you cut it, we

like to cut the countertop ⅛ inch longer than needed, then sand it down to size.

Before installing the counter, assemble any mitered corner joints. Insert the draw bolts into the prebored holes in the underside of the counters, run a thick bead of silicone caulk along the joint, then tighten the bolts to draw the seam closed.

After installing the countertop, conceal the exposed ends of the counter with end caps. Caps are available for both left- and right-hand ends.

1 *Cut the counter* to length. Then place it on top of the cabinets and use a compass to scribe the backsplash to the wall. Remove the counter and sand the backsplash to the pencil line.

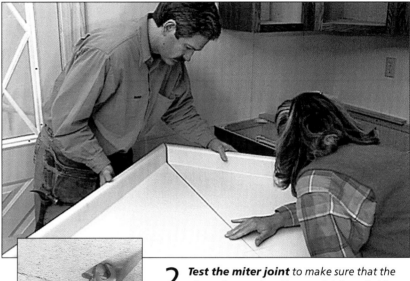

2 *Test the miter joint* to make sure that the pieces fit together. Use special threaded fasteners, called draw bolts, to pull the two mitered counter sections tightly together. Run a bead of silicone caulk along the joint before tightening the bolts.

3 *Lay a bead* of adhesive across the cabinet tops. Set the counter in place and drive screws up through the cabinet's corner blocks. To ensure that the counter is tight against the cabinets, have someone lean down on the counter as you drive each screw.

4 *Attach* the particleboard filler to the end of the counter with nails or screws, then attach the laminate end cap with contact cement. Some end caps are precoated with a heat-sensitive adhesive; apply those with a clothes iron.

Special feature

The mitered corner on this countertop has a spline to help keep the top surfaces of the countertop sections flush. The hard plastic spline is slipped into a routed groove in the ends of the counter sections before the draw bolts are tightened.

1 **Score** *the backer board with a carbide-tipped scoring knife. Snap the sheet along the scored line, then cut the mesh on the other side with a utility knife.*

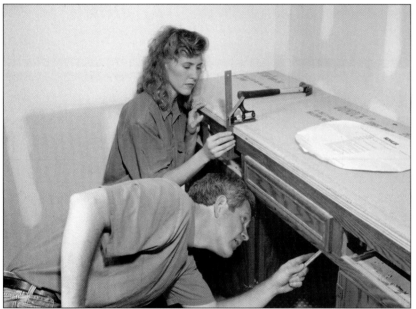

2 **Make sure** *the backer board and the plywood are perfectly aligned along the front edge. Then reach inside the cabinet and trace the sink cutout from the plywood onto the backer board.*

3 **Set** *the backer board into a bed of thinset. Fasten it to the plywood with roofing nails or backer board screws. Space the fasteners 8 inches apart along the edges and in the field.*

Ceramic Tile Counters

The first step in fabricating a tile counter is to build a rock-solid base, or substrate. A thin, weak substrate will result in cracked grout joints, popped tiles, and other hard-to-fix problems.

Building the substrate

The first layer is ¾-inch exterior-grade plywood substrate. Cut it to fit over the cabinets, making sure all joints fall over a cabinet edge. Apply adhesive to the cabinet tops, then fasten the plywood by driving screws up through the corner blocks located inside the cabinets.

Next, use the template that came with the sink to mark the sink's location on the plywood. Cut the sink opening with a jig saw.

The second layer of the substrate is ½-inch-thick cement backer board. To cut the sink opening in the backer board, first cut the pieces to size. Position the backer board over the plywood, then reach inside the cabinet and trace the outline of the sink cutout in the plywood onto the backer board.

To transfer the location of the sink opening to the other side of the backer board, turn the backer board over and drive nails through the backer board at several points along the pencil lines. Pull out the nails and score along the pencil line.

Now flip the backer board back over and, using the nail holes as guides, position the

4 **Use a 6-inch** *taping knife to spread an even coat of thinset over the seams. Embed a strip of fiberglass-mesh tape in each seam.*

template. Then mark and score the sink opening on this side of the backer board. Tap around the inside edges of the scored lines with a hammer until the cutout comes loose.

Installing the backer board

Bond the backer board to the plywood with thinset mortar. For stronger, more water-resistant thinset, mix the powder with a liquid latex additive instead of water. (Check with your supplier to make sure you're buying compatible products.)

Spread an even layer of thinset onto the plywood with a ¼-inch notched trowel. Press the backer board into the thinset and fasten it with roofing nails or special backer board screws spaced every 8 inches across the entire surface.

Use a 6-inch-wide taping knife to apply a thin layer of thinset over the seams, then embed 2-inch-wide fiberglass-mesh tape into the thinset.

Tile layout

Plan the entire tile layout before you set any tile. Lay out all the edge tiles first. Shift them back and forth until the cut pieces at the ends will be the same size.

Now lay out a few rows of field tiles, from the edge tile back to the wall. It's best to keep a full tile at the front edge of the counter and cut the ones along the wall. Also check how the cut tiles will fall around the sink. Remember, there is no one right way to lay out the tile. Just keep shifting the tile until you come up with a layout you like. When you do, use a chalkline and framing square to draw reference lines on the backer board.

Setting edge tiles

Trowel thinset along the top front edge of the backer board, but don't cover up the reference line. Next, apply a thick bead of silicone adhesive behind the front face of the edge tile and spread some extra thinset under the top surface of the edge tile. Press the tile in place. The silicone will help hold the tile in place while the thinset cures. Install all the edge tiles before moving on to the field tile.

Setting field tiles

Spread thinset onto a 2-foot-square section of backer board. Then set all the full tiles in that section. Press each tile firmly into the thinset. Give it a slight twist, then align it with its neighbors. Before moving on to the next sec-

Cutting tile

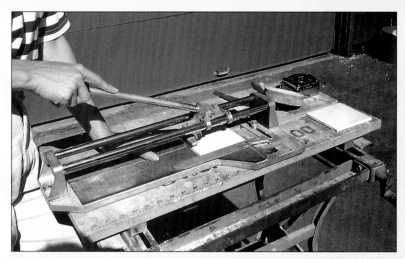

There are two steps to cutting tile with a snap cutter. First, score the tile by drawing the carbide wheel across the tile. Then press down on the handle to snap the tile. (To avoid scratching the tile, wrap masking tape around the metal wings that press down on the tile.) If the tiles aren't breaking cleanly, either the carbide wheel is dull, or the tile is too hard and must be cut on a wet saw.

Use nippers for curved cuts. Because nippers leave a ragged edge, they're only used where the cut edge will be concealed, such as by the lip of a self-rimming sink. Always take several small bites (large ones will crack the tile), and keep the jaws of the tool parallel to the cut line. Wear eye goggles as protection from sharp, flying chips.

Rent a tub saw (also called a wet saw) when you have a ton of tile to cut or cuts that will fall in a very visible area. Its diamond-impregnated blade cuts quickly and cleanly. This saw is also valuable for notching tiles. Tub saws are loud and messy so set up outside or in a garage. Always wear eye goggles and ear protection when sawing tile.

tion, double check that all the tiles you just set are sitting at the same height and that the grout joints are straight and evenly sized.

Continue working in small sections until all the full tiles have been set. When you come to the sink cutout, use a pair of nippers to trim the tiles as you go. Finally, cut all the partial tiles to fit along the wall and at the ends of the counter. Allow the thinset to cure at least 24 hours before grouting the counter. (See page 84 for information about grouting.)

5 *Dry-fit the tiles* along the edge of the counter. Shift them left or right, as necessary, to make sure that the cut tiles at each end will be the same size. Avoid using little slivers of cut tile.

6 *Silicone* adhesive holds edge tiles in place until the thinset cures. Backbutter the edge tile using silicone behind the face and thinset under the top, then press the tile onto the substrate.

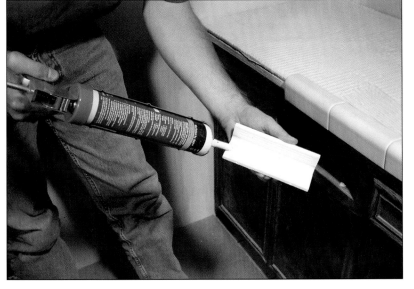

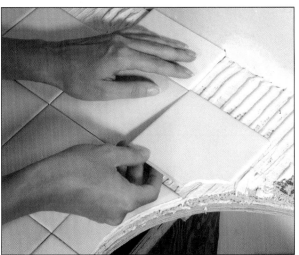

7 *Around the sink opening*, hold each tile in place and mark where it needs to be cut. Use a pair of nippers to trim the tile to the pencil line, then press it into the thinset.

8 *Use the tip* of a utility knife to carefully scrape out any thinset that may have oozed up between the tiles – it's important to clean the joints to make room for the grout.

FLOORING

Now that you've got the cabinets and counters in place, *it's time to install the kitchen's last major component: the flooring. There are few – if any – surfaces in the home that take more abuse than a kitchen floor. From muddy sneakers and high heels to splashes and spills of every description, the flooring needs to not only survive such daily onslaughts, but to endure without showing signs of wear. That's a tall order for a concrete driveway, not to mention a kitchen floor. Fortunately, there are floorcoverings that meet – and even exceed – expectations, and most of them you can install yourself.*

Installing an Underlayment

The purpose of installing a thin plywood underlayment is to provide a clean, sound surface for the new flooring. This is especially important when you install vinyl flooring, which tends to telegraph imperfections and patterns from the old flooring up through the new vinyl. However, if your existing floor is in good shape, you can lay some floorings, such as a floating plastic-laminate floor, right on top of the old floor.

The best floor underlayment is ¼-inch-thick lauan mahogany plywood. Before fastening down the plywood sheets, remove any baseboard trim. Also, be sure to lay plywood into spaces where appliances will be installed.

Secure the plywood to the floor with narrow crown staples, drywall screws, or ring-shanked nails. Place the fasteners no more than 4 inches apart along the edges and in the field. Once the plywood is securely fastened, spread leveling compound or wood putty over all the seams and fasteners. Allow the surface to dry, then sand it smooth.

1 ***Cover the old floor*** *with ¼-inch-thick lauan plywood underlayment. Notch the sheets to fit tightly around the cabinets and lay them into spaces where appliances will go.*

2 ***The nailing pattern*** *is crucial: Space fasteners no more than 4 inches apart along the seams and across the sheet (above left). Don't skimp on fasteners or you'll pay later if the underlayment buckles. Looking for a faster, easier alternative to pounding nails or driving screws? Rent an air compressor and pneumatic stapler (above right).*

3 ***Spread a thin coat*** *of wood putty over all the plywood seams and fastener heads using a 6-inch-wide drywall knife. Wide seams might require a second coat of putty to bring them flush with the surface.*

4 ***After the putty dries****, smooth the floor with a random orbit sander. Then vacuum up the dust and wipe the floor with a damp cloth or sponge mop. Be careful not to get the underlayment soaking wet.*

Sheet Vinyl

Sheet vinyl flooring is manufactured in 6- and 12-foot-wide rolls which are hundreds of feet long. That allows you to cover most average-size kitchen floors with a single, seamless sheet.

Sheet vinyl has a memory; unroll it and let it relax into a flat sheet for a day before you cut and install it. Be careful not to crease the vinyl as you unroll it. The best work space for cutting vinyl is a large, low-traffic room. Basements and garages are good choices, too. Sweep the floor before rolling out the vinyl so grit doesn't get embedded into the soft backing.

Making a template

To cut the vinyl to the exact shape of your kitchen, you must first create a paper template of the room. Make the template from a wide roll of thick paper, such as resin paper, building felt, or butcher's paper. Unroll the paper and cut it to fit from wall to wall. Trim the paper with a utility knife so it conforms to the walls, base cabinets, and all other nooks and crannies. Use duct tape to fasten the strips together. Then, every 3 feet or so, cut a small football-shaped hole out of the paper to provide openings for taping the template to the vinyl.

Once the template is completed, carefully roll it up – don't rip it! Unroll the template on top of the flooring and tape it securely in place. Then use a long steel straightedge and a sharp utility knife to cut the vinyl along the perimeter of the template.

1 **Make a paper template** of the kitchen floor out of wide strips of thick paper (above). Cut football-shaped holes in the template, then cover them with strips of 2-inch-wide duct tape (right). These will help hold the template in place when you trim the vinyl.

2 **To seam the vinyl**, overlap the sheets and tape them together. Make certain that the pattern lines printed on the sheets are precisely aligned. Plan the overlap so the seam will be hidden in a grout line.

3 **Tape the template** to the vinyl floorcovering. Then use a steel straightedge or a drywall T-square and a utility knife to cut along the edge of the template and through the flooring.

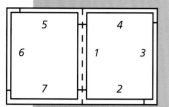

Perimeter-bonded vinyl

As its name implies, perimeter-bonded vinyl is only glued down around the edge of the room and along any seams. The rest of the flooring simply floats over the plywood underlayment.

1 **Cut the seam** before spreading any adhesive. For an inconspicuous seam, cut along the edge (not down the middle) of a pattern line or a simulated grout joint.

2 **Peel back both pieces** of the flooring and use a notched trowel to spread a 6-inch-wide stripe of adhesive onto the plywood underlayment. Center the stripe under the seam.

4 **Use a J-roller** to firmly press the seam edges into the adhesive. If any adhesive oozes out, wipe it up with a soft, damp cloth. Apply the seam sealer recommended by the flooring manufacturer.

Start by trimming the seam, if any, using a straightedge and a utility knife to slice through both layers. Then fold back one sheet from the seam, being careful not to crease it, and mark a pencil line along the edge of the second sheet (to indicate the center of the seam) before folding it back out of the way.

Use a notched trowel to spread a 6-inch-wide band of flooring adhesive on the underlayment; center it on the seam line. Lay the vinyl back down with the edges aligned to the pencil line, and press the seam into the adhesive with a J-roller.

Next, fold one sheet of flooring back onto the other, spread a 3-inch-wide band of adhesive around the edge of the room, and press the flooring into place. Repeat for the other side.

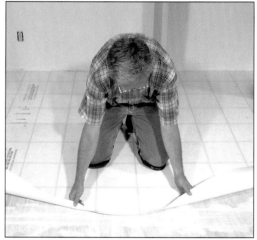

3 **Carefully lay the flooring** back down into position over the adhesive. Repeat for the second piece, then check for a tight-fitting seam.

5 **Fold back half** the vinyl and use a notched trowel to spread a 3-inch-wide band of adhesive. Carefully lay the flooring back into place and press it down. Repeat this process with the second half of the sheet.

Fully adhered vinyl

A second type of sheet vinyl, known as fully adhered flooring, is glued down with a thin coat of adhesive that's spread over the entire underlayment. There are lots of different adhesives out there, so be sure to use the one recommended by the flooring manufacturer.

Position the trimmed vinyl in the kitchen. Pull back half of the vinyl and trowel an even coat of adhesive onto the underlayment. If there's a seam, don't apply any adhesive within 18 inches of the seam line. Lay the sheet into the adhesive. Use a 100-pound floor roller to press the vinyl into the adhesive. Repeat this procedure for the other half of the vinyl.

1 ***Fold back half*** *of the sheet of flooring, then use a fine-notched trowel to spread an even coat of adhesive onto the plywood underlayment. Don't apply any adhesive within 18 inches of a seam.*

3 ***Use a floor roller*** *to firmly press the flooring into the adhesive. Start in the center of the floor and work out in all directions. Pay particular attention to any air bubbles.*

2 ***Immediately after spreading*** *out the adhesive, lay the flooring down onto the underlayment. Be very careful not to crease the flooring as you maneuver it into position.*

Next, use a long straightedge and a sharp utility knife to cut the seam. Remove the excess flooring strip. Now spread adhesive under the seam edges and use the roller to press them down. Seal the seam with the recommended seam sealer.

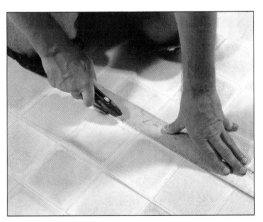

4 ***At the seam***, *cut through both flooring layers. Carefully peel back the edges and pull out the scrap trimmed off the bottom sheet. Spread adhesive under the seam with a notched trowel.*

Floor roller for tight spots

There's no question that a 100-pound floor roller is the best tool for setting the vinyl into the adhesive and chasing out any air bubbles – when you're working in a wide-open part of the room. But for tight spots, try a heavy marble rolling pin.

Setting Vinyl Tiles

Peel-and-stick vinyl tiles are easy to install, and actually kind of fun to work with. If you use the 12-inch-square size, the job goes pretty quickly, too. You won't need much in the way of tools, but treat yourself to a good pair of knee pads.

The first thing to do is to make absolutely sure that the underlayment is dry and completely free of any dust or dirt. Next, find the exact center of the room and snap two perpendicular chalk lines. Start laying the tiles in the center of the room and fill one quadrant of the floor at a time. As you set each tile, press it firmly into place. Work back and forth between the lines until you reach the walls. At that point, you'll need to cut tiles to fit, but save all the cutting until all four quadrants are filled.

To cut the tiles, you'll need a sharp utility knife, a framing square, and a scrap piece of plywood for a cutting board so you don't accidentally mar the new floor.

To mark a straight cut, lay the tile on top of the last full tile. Place another tile on top, hold it against the wall, and mark the middle tile where the top tile overlaps it.

After dividing the floor into four equal quadrants, start laying tiles in the center. Work back and forth between the perpendicular layout lines. Fill one quadrant before moving on to the next.

1 **To notch a tile** around a base cabinet, place it on top of the tile that's nearest the corner. Use a felt-tip pen to mark where it meets the front edge of the toekick.

2 **Then shift the tile** to the front of the base cabinet. Hold it tightly against the edge of the previously installed tiles and mark where it meets the side of the cabinet.

3 **Lay a framing square** on top of the tile and align it with the two pen marks. Draw lines to mark the notch, then cut it out with a utility knife.

Plastic-Laminate Planks

Plastic-laminate flooring was invented in Sweden during the early 1980s and brought to North America in 1994. It's available in tongue-and-groove planks and square tiles. The flooring is only about ¼ inch thick so it's ideal for a kitchen remodel where you don't want to raise the floor too much.

But perhaps best of all, it's easy to install because it's a floating floor. The planks aren't attached to the underlayment at all, they're simply glued together. Plus, it can be laid directly over virtually any existing floor.

To start, remove any baseboard trim and roll out a layer of ⅛-inch-thick foam underlayment. Next, dry-fit (no glue) the first row of planks along the wall, making sure the tongues stick out into the room. If the wall is wavy or has any major irregularities, use a compass to scribe the planks, then cut them with a jig saw.

1 **Unroll polyethylene foam** underlayment across the old floor. Butt the seams, don't overlap them. The ⅛-inch-thick foam muffles sound, provides thermal insulation, and evens out imperfections in the old floor.

2 **Lay out the first row** of planks with the grooved edges pressed against the wall. Use a compass to transfer any irregularities in the wall to the flooring. Cut along the scribed pencil line with a jig saw.

3 **Slip ¼-inch-thick spacers** between the walls and the planks to create expansion room for the flooring. Leave spacers in until all the flooring has been laid. The gaps will be hidden by the baseboard.

4 **Cut the last plank** in the row to fit against the wall; be sure to allow for a spacer at the end. A power miter saw (shown) cuts cleanly, but a hand saw also works well. Put the cut end against the wall.

Cutting waste

When ordering plastic-laminate flooring, always get an additional five percent to cover waste and mistakes (hey, they happen).

To keep waste to a minimum, start each new row with the leftover piece cut from the last plank in the previous row. However, if the leftover piece is less than 8 inches long, don' t use it. Instead, start the new row with either a full or half plank.

Gluing the planks

Dry-fit all the planks for the first three rows; be sure to place spacers along the walls. Then carefully separate the planks and apply glue to the grooves in the ends of the planks in the first row. Don't glue the grooves that face the wall. As you pull the joints closed, glue should ooze out onto the top surface. If it doesn't, you're not using enough glue. Immediately clean off the excess glue with a damp cloth.

Start the second row by applying a continuous bead of glue to the grooves in the end and edge of the first plank. Set it in place alongside the first row and use a hammer and block to carefully tap the joint closed. Wipe up the excess glue and check that the two

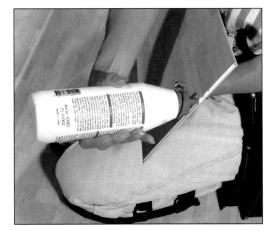

5 *Apply a continuous bead* of glue to the grooves milled in the end and edge of the planks. Don't skimp on the glue. A pint of glue is enough for about 100 square feet of flooring.

6 *Protect the edge* of the plank with a tapping block, then use a hammer to strike the block and close up the tongue-and-groove joint. Never hit the edge of an unprotected plank – you'll damage the tongue.

7 *A thin bead of glue* will squeeze up onto the surface after you tap the plank into position – if you used the correct amount of glue. Immediately remove the excess glue with a damp cloth. Rinse the cloth often in clean water.

planks are locked tightly together. Finish gluing the remaining planks in the second and third rows. Then wait at least one hour for the glue to cure before proceeding.

Notching planks for a perfect fit

As you work your way across the floor, you'll eventually run into an obstruction that'll require you to notch a plank. The best tools for cutting the notches are a jig saw or hand saw. If you use a jig saw, place the plank face down to avoid chipping the laminate surface. When using a hand saw, position the plank face up.

At a doorway, you'll need to trim off the bottom of the casing (the vertical molding at each side of the doorway opening) so the flooring can fit underneath. Lay a plank face down on top of the foam underlayment beside the casing. Place a hand saw flat on the plank and use it as a guide as you cut through the molding.

Chances are you'll also have to install transition molding across the threshold at each doorway to protect and conceal the edge of the plank. Most flooring manufacturers offer a variety of aluminum and wood transition moldings.

8 *To notch a plank* to fit around an obstruction, use a jig saw fitted with a fine-toothed blade. Clamp the plank face down. That way, any chipping will occur on the bottom surface. If you use a hand saw to cut the notches, clamp the plank face up.

9 *Dry-fit the notched plank* to make sure it fits. At a doorway, the plank must slide underneath the door casing and fit tightly into the slot in the transition molding that's installed across the threshold.

10 *Use a pull bar* to close the end joint on the last plank in each row when there's not enough room to use a hammer and tapping block. Hook the bar onto the end of the plank and tap the raised flange to draw the joint closed.

11 *Install* the first three rows of flooring, then wait an hour for the glue to cure. The delay allows all the planks to solidify into a slab and not shift out of position as you install the next rows.

12 *Measure and mark* planks that must be cut to fit around base cabinets. When laying out the cut lines, don't forget to leave a ¼-inch expansion space between the plank and base cabinet.

13 *After checking* that the notched plank fits, apply the glue and slip it into place. Be careful not to wrinkle or rip the foam underlayment. Then tighten up the joints using a hammer and the metal pull bar.

Fitting the last row

When you get to the last row of planks, you'll probably have to rip them down to size. You could measure and mark each and every plank, but there is an easier way. Lay a plank directly on top of the next to last row; be sure its tongue faces the wall. Then place a scrap piece of plank on top with its tongue touching the wall. Now, hold a pencil against the grooved edge and slide the scrap piece along the wall to mark the plank below; any irregularities in the wall will be transferred to the pencil line. If the line is pretty straight, go ahead and rip the plank with a circular saw. For more complex cuts, use a jig saw.

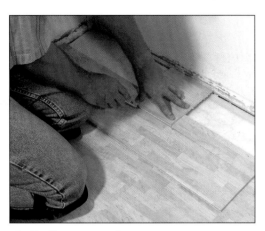

14 *Use a scrap* piece *of flooring as a marking gauge for scribing the planks to fit into the last row. Slide the scrap piece along the wall and mark the plank below.*

15 *Rip the plank* to *the proper width by cutting along the pencil line with a circular saw. To minimize chipping, use a thin-kerf, carbide-tipped blade.*

16 *Install* baseboard *molding around the room to conceal the ¼-inch expansion space. Drive the finishing nails into wall studs which are typically located 16 inches on center.*

Options for a real wood floor

If you're looking to add a real wood floor to your kitchen, you're in luck. Several manufacturers offer replacement wood flooring that's specifically designed for remodeling jobs. Unlike traditional ¾-inch-thick hardwood flooring, these floors are thin, prefinished, and easy to install.

They're available in two styles: solid-wood strips and engineered-wood planks. Solid-wood strips are individual boards of random widths and lengths that come as thin as 5/16 inch. They can be set in a bed of mastic or shot down with a pneumatic stapler, as shown below.

Engineered-wood planks are made similar to plywood and have at least three layers: a hardwood top veneer that's about ⅛ inch thick, a core of wood crossbands that run perpendicular to the top, and a bottom veneer. Each plank is about ½ inch thick x 7 inches wide x 8 feet long. The planks can be nailed or glued down, but most of the time they're simply glued together to create a floating floor.

Ceramic Tile

Once upon a time, not so very long ago, setting a ceramic-tile floor was a job best left to a pro. It was simply too risky, too complicated, and much too messy for the average homeowner to undertake. But now, thanks to several new time- and labor-saving materials and techniques, any competent do-it-yourselfer can lay a tile floor.

Laying the substrate

The first – and most important – step is to create a smooth, rock-solid substrate, or base, for the tile. If there's any flex or bounce in the subfloor, you'll have tiles cracking and popping loose in no time.

The traditional way to create a stable base is to set the tiles into a thick bed of mortar, commonly called mud. It's a great system except that it's labor intensive and it significantly raises the floor; the mud bed alone is often a full inch thick.

The modern method is to spread a layer of thinset mortar over the existing floor and then fasten down an underlayment of cement backer board. Standard backer board is ½ inch thick, but ¼-inch sheets are also available for keeping the finished height of the floor as low as possible. Once the backer board is nailed down, the seams must be finished with thinset and mesh tape.

1 *After scoring the backer board along the cut line with a carbide-tipped scoring knife, snap the board to break it. Then use a utility knife to slice through the fiberglass mesh on the back.*

2 *To fasten the backer board in place, first spread a coat of thinset onto the existing floor with a ¼-inch notched trowel. Work in manageable sections so the thinset won't dry out.*

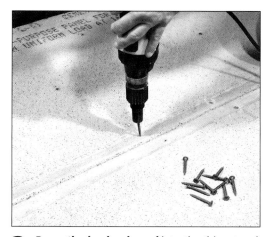

3 *Press the backer board into the thinset and secure it with roofing nails or special backer board screws; place one fastener every 8 inches along all four edges and across the entire surface.*

4 *Use a 6-inch taping knife to spread a layer of thinset over all the seams between the backer board sheets. Then cover the seams with 2-inch-wide fiberglass-mesh tape.*

Working with thinset mortar

To ensure a good bond between the backer board and the thinset, fasten down the board immediately after spreading the thinset. If you wait too long, the thinset will skin over and form a weak bond. To extend the working time of the thinset, mix it with cold water.

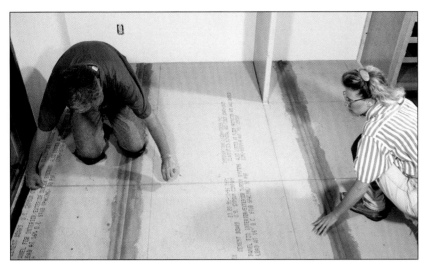

1 ***Snap layout lines*** *onto the backer board with a chalk line. Use a framing square to make sure that the grid lines are perfectly square. Each grid section should be sized to accommodate about two square feet of full tiles and the grout spaces between them. Check the grid size by dry-laying tiles in one section.*

To beat or not to beat

At one time, tile setters had to beat tiles into the mortar with a rubber mallet to ensure a good bond. But the makers of today's high-tech adhesives and thinset mortars claim that it's no longer necessary to beat tiles.

We've adopted a why-risk-it policy and still beat in the tiles. It only takes a few minutes and helps level any tiles that may be a little higher than their neighbors.

Laying out the tile pattern

Once the seams of the backer board have cured overnight, you can start tiling. But where do you begin? Unfortunately, there's no one specific answer. Start by identifying the focal point of the kitchen. Look for the one feature that draws your eye when you enter the room; it's typically the primary sink, but the focal point might be a window, work island, or range.

Layout lines

The best-looking tile jobs are visually balanced, meaning that the cut tiles around the edge of the floor are the same size. Nothing upsets a tile pattern more than setting a row of full tiles along one wall with a row of tile slivers along the facing wall. To achieve a balanced pattern, start by dry-laying a row of tiles from the center of the focal point out in both directions toward the walls. Don't forget to leave spaces between the tiles for grout joints.

When you get to the walls and can no longer fit full tiles, measure the remaining spaces. If necessary, shift the row of tiles a little to the left or right so that the border tiles will be of equal size. To determine the tile pattern between the other two walls, repeat this process with a row of tiles perpendicular to the first row. Use these two lines of tile as reference points for snapping a grid of layout lines onto the floor.

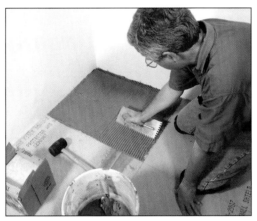

2 ***Start in the far corner*** *of the kitchen and spread thinset with the smooth edge of a trowel. Turn the tool around and comb out the thinset with the notched edge. The resulting ridges help form a strong bond.*

3 ***Set the first tile*** *in the corner of the chalk-line grid. Carefully align it to both lines. Firmly press the tile into the thinset, then lightly twist it back and forth to ensure full contact between the tile and the mortar.*

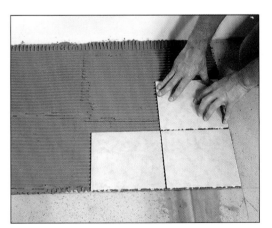

4 ***Continue setting tiles*** *to fill the section. Be sure to leave gaps between them for grout. Work steadily at this point. If you dawdle, even for just a few minutes, the thinset will skin over and the tiles won't adhere properly.*

Floor tiling sequence

Begin by troweling thinset across a grid section in the far corner of the room. Be careful not to obscure the chalk lines. Align the first tile with two intersecting lines and gently press it into the thinset with a slight twisting motion. Lay the other full tiles within the section, then tap them with a rubber mallet to set them into the thinset. Clean off any thinset that may have squeezed up between the tiles. Now check to make sure the tiles are all sitting at the same height and that the spacing between the tiles is uniform in width and perfectly straight.

Cutting tile

Mark any tiles that must be cut to fit along the wall – again, don't forget to allow for the grout joints. Trim the tiles with a manual snap cutter (it can be rented at any tool rental shop and most tile stores). Lay a tile flat on the cutter, lower the handle, and draw the carbide wheel across the tile's glazed surface. Then push down on the handle to snap the tile in two. Smooth the sharp edge with a rub stone. When installing the tiles, be certain to face the cut edges toward the wall.

5 *No need to measure* when you have to cut a tile to fit along a wall. Instead, lay the tile in place and mark where it butts up against the adjacent tile. Make sure to allow for a grout joint between tiles and an expansion space at the wall.

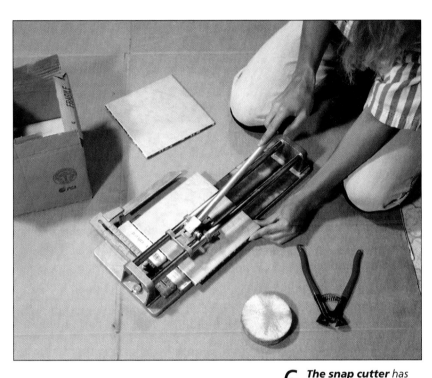

6 *The snap cutter* has no equal when it comes to cutting ceramic tile quickly, quietly, and neatly. Pull the handle to draw the carbide scoring wheel across the tile, then press down to snap it. Be sure to wear safety glasses.

Skip the spacers

Some floor tiles have tiny edge bumps, called lugs, that automatically create uniform grout joints. For tiles without lugs, you can buy tile spacers (small cross-shaped rubber pieces that you place between the tiles). They're a good idea in theory, but in reality, tile spacers don't work very well. The reason: Even tiles from the same batch will vary slightly in size because they shrink at different rates when fired in the kiln. The grout joints must compensate for these minute variations in tile size.

We don't use spacers with floor tiles and instead trust the layout lines snapped onto the floor. You can use a homemade reference guide, called a story pole, to check the tile alignment as you go (see photo at left).

Grouting

Grout is the material that you pack into the joints between the tiles. Its purpose, of course, is to prevent water from seeping under the tiles. You'll find both sanded and non-sanded grout at your local home center. Use non-sanded grout for joints that are ⅛ inch wide or less, and sanded grout for wider joints.

Mixing grout

Grout comes either plain or fortified with an additive, such as latex or acrylic resin. Additives improve the grout's water resistance and make it much more resilient and flexible. Mix plain grout with a liquid latex additive instead of water. Fortified grout already contains a powdered additive, so go ahead and mix it with plain water. After you mix up a batch of grout, let it sit and slake for 10 to 15 minutes. That'll give the liquid time to completely soak into all the dry ingredients. Then gently mix it once more to dissolve any remaining lumps.

1 *You can begin grouting* 48 hours after setting the last tile. Force grout into the gaps between the tiles with a grout float. Hold the float at a 30-degree angle to pack the joints with grout. Switch to a 90-degree angle to scrape off the excess.

The right tool for the job

That's no ordinary sponge we use to clean tile. A grout sponge has rounded edges that are less likely than squared edges to drag grout out of the joints when you're wiping off the excess. The rounded edges are also handy for smoothing the joints.

2 *After grouting about* 15 to 20 square feet of tile, go back and clean off the remaining grout with a damp sponge. Use slow, steady strokes on the final cleaning pass. Make only one stroke with each side of the sponge before rinsing it in cool, clean water.

3 *Tool* the grout joints by gently drawing the rounded edge of a damp grout sponge along the joints. The grout should be slightly below the tile, but be careful not to drag too much grout out of the joints.

Applying grout

Force the grout into the joints with a rubber grout float. Hold the float at a 30-degree angle to the floor and swipe it diagonally across the tiles. To remove the excess grout, make another pass with the float held almost perpendicular to the tile. Wait about 10 to 15 minutes, then wipe off the excess grout with a damp (not wet) sponge. When a light haze appears on the tiles, buff it off with a clean, dry cloth.

4 *After a cloudy haze* appears on the tiles, buff the surface with a dry cloth. If you come across spots of dried grout that won't come off, try a plastic scouring pad.

FINAL HOOKUPS

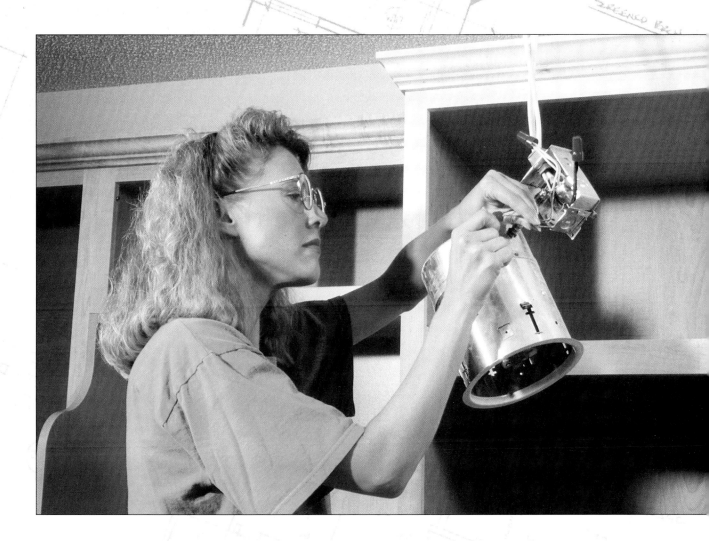

The final phase, called the trim-out or wrap-up stage, *is a series of small jobs that includes hooking up the sink, installing appliances, wiring light fixtures, and putting on the cabinet doors, drawers, and knobs. Although this may seem to be an assortment of unrelated tasks, there is a logical work sequence to follow.*

You'll be able to do most of the work yourself, but call in a pro for complicated or potentially dangerous jobs (like running a gas line or connecting new circuits to the main electrical panel). Finally, don't forget to schedule a final inspection of the completed kitchen.

Installing the Sink

The first step to finishing a kitchen is installing the faucet and sink. Many of the other appliances and fixtures (including the garbage disposer, dishwasher, hot-water dispenser, and ice maker) can't be installed until the sink is hooked up.

Always install the faucet, spray hose, and other sink-mounted accessories before setting the sink into the countertop. This will save you the trouble of having to tighten the retaining nuts later while laying flat on your back inside the cabinet – not a fun job. You can work right on the floor, but it's more comfortable with the sink propped up on a base cabinet or sawhorses.

Fastening the faucet

Faucets come in many different styles, but they all get installed basically the same way. Start by slipping the baseplate gasket over the faucet tailpieces (the two inlet supply tubes that hang down from the faucet). Insert the tailpieces through the center hole in the sink. If the faucet requires three holes, slip the tailpieces into the outer holes; the center hole is for the spray-hose stubout. Screw mounting nuts over the tailpieces from below. Before tightening the nuts, be sure the faucet is parallel with the sink's rear edge.

The plumbing under a kitchen sink consists of small-diameter water-supply lines and larger drain pipes. This illustration also includes an electric hot-water dispenser and a garbage disposer. (Note that the dishwasher drain line runs to an air gap, then to the disposer.)

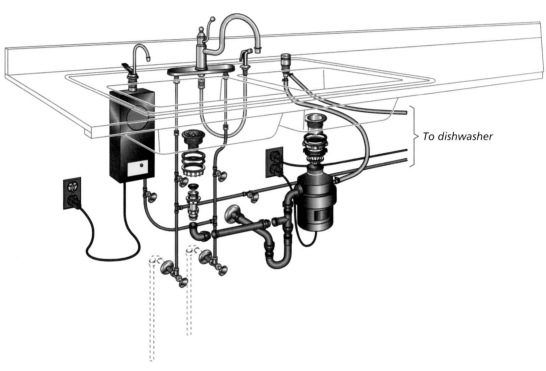

To dishwasher

1 *Attach two shut-off valves* to each riser in-side the sink cabinet. The four valves provide hot and cold water to the faucet, hot water to the dishwasher, and cold water to the ice maker.

2 *After fastening the faucet* to the sink, con-nect the flexible water-supply tubes to the brass fittings at the ends of the copper tailpieces. Be sure to use two wrenches when tightening the threaded fittings.

3 *The holes in the sink deck can accommodate a wide range of accessories. Here, we're installing the mounting base for a liquid soap dispenser. A refillable bottle will hang below the sink.*

4 *Run beads of silicone adhesive around the sink cutout, then spread them with a putty knife.*

5 *A cast-iron sink is extremely heavy; have someone help you lift it into place. Leave out the strainers so you'll be able to reach through the drain holes for a firm grip.*

Next, secure the hot- and cold-water supply tubes to the ends of the tailpieces. There are many kinds of supply tubes available, but we like using polymer tubing sheathed in braided stainless steel. It's flexible, virtually indestructible, and comes with threaded fittings already attached so there's no cutting or assembly; you just screw them in place.

If there's a pull-out spray hose, attach its threaded base to the mounting hole on the sink deck and connect the hose end to the stubout under the faucet. Install any other sink-mounted accessories in the remaining holes. If you run out of holes and need to install an air gap, mount it into the countertop. (An air gap is a small vacuum breaker that prevents dirty water from backing up into the dishwasher; it's code-required in many areas.)

At this stage, you can also install the strainers into the drain holes. However, when installing a heavy cast-iron sink, we prefer to install the strainers later so that we can grab the sink by the drain holes and hoist it into place.

Setting the sink

Installing a self-rimming, cast-iron sink is a snap. Run two beads of silicone adhesive around the edge of the cutout in the counter, spread them with a putty knife, then lower the sink into place. Make sure that it's centered in the opening and parallel with the front edge of the counter. Wipe off any adhesive that oozes out.

A stainless steel sink, either a self-rimming or surface-mount style, comes with metal clips and retaining screws for securing it to the counter. Use a clip on each side of the sink corners and every 8 inches in between. Tighten each screw a little at a time until they're all snug.

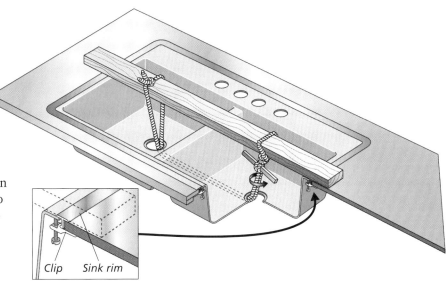

Clip   Sink rim

When installing a flush-mount or an undermount sink, use a 2x4 and a length of rope to suspend the sink in the opening. Then reach up from underneath and hook the metal fastening clips to the perimeter or the sink rim. Tighten the retaining screws on the clips to draw the sink tight against the counter.

Plumbing hookups

The procedure for plumbing a kitchen sink has gotten a little complicated over the years. Most modern kitchens have a double-bowl sink, garbage disposer, and dishwasher – and all those components come together inside the sink cabinet. In addition, some ice makers get hooked up under the sink.

The first step is to connect the flexible water-supply tubes from the faucet to the appropriate hot- and cold-water shut-off valves on the risers. Thread the fittings onto the valves by hand and tighten them with an open-end or adjustable wrench.

Now, take a blob of plumber's putty and roll it between your palms to form a ½-inch-diameter rope that's about a foot long. Wrap the putty around the flange on the underside of the strainer, then set it into the drain hole. From underneath, add the gaskets and thread on the large spud nut. Tighten the nut with groove-joint pliers until most of the plumber's putty squeezes out from under the flange inside the sink. Wipe off the excess putty with a damp, clean cloth.

The next step is to install the garbage disposer into the remaining drain hole (see the next page for details). If you're not installing a disposer, trim out the other drain hole with a strainer, as described above.

After the strainer and disposer (or two strainers) are attached to the sink, you can start putting together the drain assembly. At

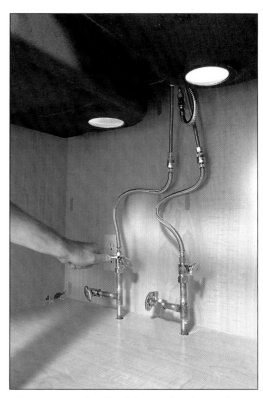

6 *Connect the flexible* supply tubes to the appropriate hot- and cold-water valves on the risers. Carefully thread the fittings on by hand – beware of crossed threads – then finish tightening them with a wrench.

one time, drains used to be plumbed almost exclusively with chrome-plated brass pipe. However, PVC (white) plastic pipe is more durable and much easier to install.

7 *Wrap plumber's putty* all the way around the strainer flange before installing the strainer into the drain hole. Don't skimp on the putty or it'll fail to form a watertight seal.

8 *Insert the strainer* through the drain hole and slip on the rubber gasket (sometimes there's a paper gasket, too). Tighten the spud nut until most of the putty oozes out.

Garbage Disposers

Generally speaking, any kitchen sink can be equipped with a garbage disposer, but codes vary widely so check with the building department.

Start by inserting the disposer's sink flange into the drain hole of the smallest or shallowest sink bowl. Slip the two-part mounting ring onto the flange from below and tighten the screws.

Next, attach the discharge tube to the hole in the side of the disposer. Directly above the discharge tube is a short pipe, called a dishwasher nipple. If you're putting in a dishwasher, knock out the plug from the nipple with a screwdriver.

Most disposers come without a power

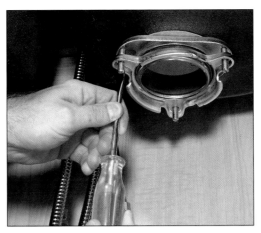

1 ***Secure the flange*** *to the drain hole by tightening the screws on the mounting rings. Some disposers require a bead of plumber's putty under the flange, while others come with a neoprene gasket.*

2 ***Place the L-shaped*** *plastic discharge tube over the hole in the side of the disposer; point it downward. Attach the tube with screws driven through its metal flange.*

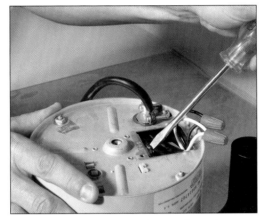

3 ***Remove the access plate*** *and attach a 12-gauge appliance cord. Use one twist-on wire connector to join the two white wires, and another to join the black wires. Secure the green wire under the grounding screw.*

cord. They must be either hard-wired directly to a dedicated wall switch, or plugged into an outlet controlled by a switch. (Again, check the code requirements in your town.) During the electrical rough-in phase, we put an outlet inside the sink cabinet so we just had to wire the disposer with a length of 12-gauge appliance cord that had a three-prong grounded plug attached.

To install the disposer, lift it into place and rotate the lower mounting ring clockwise until it locks onto the unit. Now build the drain assembly out of PVC pipe and fittings.

4 ***Rotate the lower*** *mounting ring clockwise to lock the disposer into position. Make sure the discharge tube is facing in the proper direction for connecting to the drain pipe.*

5 ***There's no such thing*** *as a typical drain assembly, but a two-bowl sink with disposer should resemble this setup. Start by connecting the horizontal trap arm to the stub-out in the wall.*

Ice Makers

If your refrigerator is equipped with an automatic ice maker or chilled water dispenser (or both), it must be connected to a cold-water supply line. Make the connection with either a length of ¼-inch-diameter soft copper tubing or flexible plastic tubing.

Begin by choosing the most direct route for the tubing. In most cases, it's best to bore holes through the inside of the base cabinets and run the tubing from the rear of the refrigerator to a shut-off valve under the sink. Another option is to bore a hole through the floor behind the refrigerator, feed the tubing down into the basement or crawl space, and tap into an existing cold-water pipe with a T-fitting and shut-off valve.

1 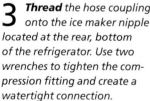 **After boring holes** through the cabinet sides, start at the refrigerator space and feed the flexible tubing through the holes. Be careful not to twist or kink the tubing.

Attaching the tubing

Use a ⅜-inch-diameter drill bit to bore a hole through the side of each base cabinet that's between the refrigerator and sink. Then, starting at the refrigerator alcove, feed the tubing end through the holes in the cabinets. Once the end reaches the valve under the sink, make sure you have at least 6 feet of extra tubing at the refrigerator end. The excess is needed to make the final connection to the refrigerator; it also allows you to roll out the appliance for cleaning and inspection.

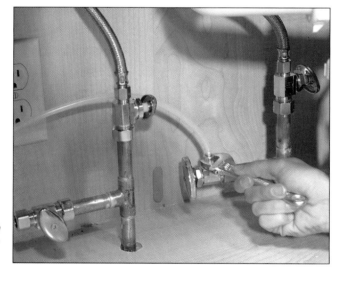

2 **Use** a compression fitting to attach the tubing to the shut-off valve on the cold-water riser. Leave some slack in the tubing so it doesn't kink at the fitting.

Connect the end of the tubing to the shut-off valve under the sink with a compression fitting. Slip the coupling nut over the tubing end, then slide on the compression ring. Thread the coupling nut onto the valve and tighten it with a wrench.

At the refrigerator end, use a compression fitting to attach a threaded female hose coupling (similar to the kind used on garden hoses) to the tubing. Tighten the coupling onto the ice maker nipple at the rear of the refrigerator.

3 **Thread** the hose coupling onto the ice maker nipple located at the rear, bottom of the refrigerator. Use two wrenches to tighten the compression fitting and create a watertight connection.

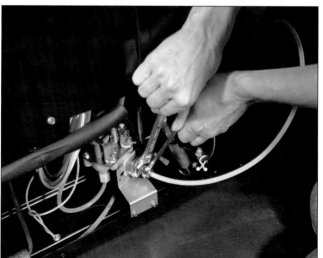

Dishwashers

Installing a dishwasher isn't a particularly difficult job, but it does take time since there are three different hookups: drainage, electricity, and hot-water supply. If you worked carefully during the mechanical rough-in stage, this installation will go smoothly.

If the local code requires an air gap, install it now. Otherwise, when it comes time to hook up the dishwasher, remember to loop the drain hose up as high as possible inside the cabinet before connecting it to the garbage disposer or drain assembly.

Mechanical connections

Start by boring a hole in the sink cabinet large enough for the drain hose, water-supply tube, and electrical cable. Position the dishwasher near, but not in, the space provided for it. (Put down cardboard to protect the flooring.) Pop open the access panel located below the dishwasher door, then slide the cable, drain hose, and supply tubing underneath (all these connections can be made from the front of the dishwasher). Slip the flexible drain hose onto the dishwasher's discharge fitting and secure it with a clamp.

1 ***Remove the front access panel***, *then push the drain hose onto the discharge fitting. If the fit is too tight, lubricate the hose end with a little liquid detergent. Secure the connection with a clamp.*

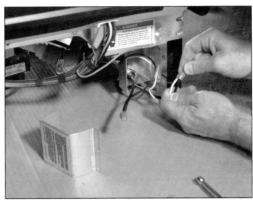

2 ***Unscrew the metal cover*** *from the dishwasher's junction box. Push the power cord into the box and join the wires with twist-on wire connectors. Attach the green grounding wire to the screw inside the box.*

3 ***Cut*** *an extra-long piece of copper tubing to serve as the water-supply line. Pass it through the hole in the sink cabinet. Be sure it extends out far enough to reach the dishwasher.*

Next, connect the power cable to the dishwasher. A dishwasher can either be hardwired to a dedicated 20-amp circuit or wired with a 12-gauge appliance cord and plugged into an outlet on a dedicated 20-amp circuit. In some areas, codes allow the dishwasher and disposer to share a single 20-amp circuit, but it's more typical to install a split-circuit receptacle.

In either case, open the junction box at the front of the dishwasher. Gently unfold the loose wire ends and feed the cable end into the box. Use twist-on wire connectors to make white-to-white, and black-to-black connections. (Exception: If the cable has two black wires, join one of them to the dishwasher's white wire.) Attach the green wire to the grounding screw inside the metal box.

Next, feed the copper tubing through the hole into the sink cabinet (most dishwashers accept either 3/8- or 1/2-inch-diameter tubing). Use a compression fitting to attach the tubing to the shut-off valve on the hot-water riser.

Final hookups

Slide the dishwasher all the way under the counter. At the same time, have someone guide the drain hose and electrical cable into the sink cabinet. Work slowly to avoid kinking the hose or pinching the copper tubing under the dishwasher.

Use a compression fitting to join the copper tubing to the L-fitting protruding from the dishwasher's water valve. Under the sink, connect the drain hose to the air gap or directly to the disposer. If there's no air gap or disposer, attach the hose to the waste-T tailpiece under the sink. If the dishwasher is wired with an appliance cord, plug it into the wall outlet.

Next, level the dishwasher by adjusting its two front feet. Secure it to the underside of the countertop by driving screws up through the metal tabs located at the top of the dishwasher.

Finally, turn on the water and electricity and run the dishwasher through a test cycle. Turn on the faucet and disposer, too. Check all plumbing connections under the dishwasher and sink for leaks.

Stabilizing a dishwasher

After leveling the dishwasher – but before you drive any screws through the mounting tabs – check to make sure the appliance is sitting flat on the floor. Lean inside the dishwasher and push down on opposite corners. Then press down on the other two opposing corners. If you detect even a little wobble, readjust the leveling feet.

4 *A compression fitting* connects the copper supply tubing to the shut-off valve on the hot-water riser. Tighten the coupling nut with an open-end wrench.

5 *Use a wrench* to turn the two leveling feet and raise the dishwasher until the mounting tabs touch the underside of the counter. Then check to make sure the unit is level and plumb.

6 *Open the door* and locate the two metal mounting tabs at the top of the dishwasher. Drive a short screw through the hole in each tab and into the underside of the countertop.

Light Fixtures

The main wiring for the kitchen's lighting was done during the rough-in stage. All you need to do now is make the electrical connections to the light fixtures and secure each fixture.

Flush-mounted ceiling fixtures and pendant (hanging) lights are secured to an electrical box. Flush-mounted models are typically screwed to a metal strap attached to the box, or they fit onto a hollow nipple screwed into the strap. Pendant lights are also hung from the box with a nipple; a decorative canopy hides the junction box.

Recessed fixtures

If you wired in recessed cans during the rough-in stage, then just screw in the light bulb and attach the trim kit (that's the decorative ring that goes against the ceiling). You can also install recessed can lights in an existing ceiling by using retrofit fixtures.

Cut a hole in the ceiling for each fixture. Reach up and pull down the electrical cable. If there are two or more lights wired in a series, there will be two cables. Each recessed light has its own junction box. Pass both cables into the box, tighten the cable clamps, and use twist-on wire connectors to join like-color wires. Connect the bare (ground) wire inside the box to the bare wire coming from each cable.

Attach the trim-kit baffle to the recessed fixture. This particular model hooks onto the interior of the housing with two springs. Other styles clip on with long, rigid wires.

Pull the cables *down from the ceiling and connect them to same-color wires inside the fixture's junction box. Unless the fixture is rated for contact with insulation, keep any ceiling insulation three inches away from it.*

Screw the fluorescent fixture to the upper cabinet. Join the wires with twist-on wire connectors.

Adding a ceiling fan

A ceiling fan with light kit is a smart addition to any kitchen. However, you can't simply remove a ceiling-mounted light and hang the fan from the existing junction box. To support the extra weight of a ceiling fan you must attach a 2x6 brace between the joists above the box. Then drive ¼-inch lag screws or number 12 wood screws through the fan's mounting plate, through the junction box, and into the brace. If there's no access to the ceiling, install an expanding steel fan bracket.

Secure the wooden fan blades to the rotating metal arms with the screws provided. If rubber bushings were also included, place one on each screw before driving it.

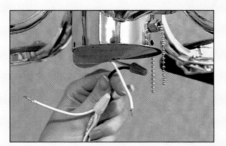

Ceiling fans come prewired so that all the electrical connections can be made with twist-on wire connectors. Read the installation instructions for the color-coded wiring sequence.

Carefully hold each glass shade into the socket housing and hand tighten the knurled locking screws. Don't overtighten the screws or you'll crack the shade.

Now lift the fixture into the hole and firmly press it to the ceiling until the retaining clips lock onto the drywall edge. Put in a bulb and attach the trim kit.

Task lighting

The most popular task-light fixtures are the slim, undercabinet models used to illuminate countertops. Installation varies according to the fixture, but there is a basic procedure. Pull the cable through the access hole and cable clamp in the fixture's mounting plate, then screw the plate to the underside of the upper cabinet. Make the wire connections with twist-on wire connectors, attach the fixture to the mounting plate, and install the bulbs.

Low voltage hockey puck lights are available in surface-mount and recessed versions; a few models allow for both installation options. Make sure you have the right fixture for your installation.

To install the fixture, use a hole saw to cut a hole through the soffit or cabinet top. (Use a spade bit for a surface mount installation since you only need a hole big enough to pull the wires through.) Pull down the low-voltage wire, plug it into the fixture, push the fixture into the hole, then snap on the trim kit. Follow the manufacturer's directions for installing the transformer.

Use a hole saw and drill to cut the hole for a recessed halogen hockey puck. Move the wire above the hole out of the way before sawing through.

Plug the low-voltage wire into the halogen fixture, then push it up into the hole. Some models must be fastened with screws, others simply snap into place.

The end is in sight. Install all the adjustable shelves, roll-out trays, recycling bins, and other interior cabinet hardware. Then hang the doors, slide in the drawers, and attach the pulls or knobs. Now call to schedule the final inspection.

Index